SKILL DEVELOPMENT IN INDIA

SKILL DEVELOPMENT IN INDIA

Aspirations and Achievements

P. Satyanarayana

SHIPRA

Rs. 795, US$ 39.75

ISBN: 978-93-86262-60-8

First Published in India in 2018

Skill Development in India

Published by:
SHIPRA PUBLICATIONS
LG 18-19, Pankaj Central Market,
I.P. Ext., Patparganj, Delhi 110092, India
91 11 47322068, 9650028065, 9810522367
Email: info@shiprapublication.com
Website: www.shiprapublication.com

Contents

1

Introduction

Equipping the workforce with the skills required for the jobs of today and those of tomorrow is a strategic concern in the national growth and development outlooks of all countries. The globalization of markets is accelerating the diffusion of technology and the pace of innovation. New occupations are emerging and replacing others. Within each occupation, required skills and competencies are evolving, as the knowledge content of production processes and services rising. A major challenge in all countries, particularly developing nations, is simultaneously to enhance the responsiveness of education and training systems to these changes in skill requirements and to improve access to training and skills development. Each country's prosperity depends on how many of its people are in work and how productive they are, which in turn rests on the skills they have and how effectively those skills are used. Skills are a foundation of decent work.

The cornerstones of a policy framework for developing a suitably skilled workforce, in terms of ILO, are:

- board availability of good quality education as a foundation for future training;
- chose matching of skills supply to the needs of enterprises and labor markets;
- enabling works and enterprises to adjust to changes in technology and markets; and
- anticipating and preparing for the skills needs of the future.

Initiatives of ILO, OECD, European Commission

Sometime back, governments, workers and employers representatives at ILO Conference adopted a set of conclusions on skills for improved productivity, employment growth and development. OCED produced several major reports on vocational education and training and on school-to-work situations. The European Commission embarked on a New Skills for New Jobs Initiatives. The World Bank proposed a new skills strategy geared to employability strategy and productivity.

Skills Enhance People's Capacities

Skills development enhances both people's capacities to work and their opportunities at work, offering more scope for creativity and satisfaction at work. The future prosperity of any Country depends ultimately on the number of persons in employment and how productive they are work. A rich literature exists on the links between education, skills, productivity and economic growth.

India's Initiatives

India's initiatives in skills development began during the 11th Five Year Plan period. For the first time, the Plan provides a framework to address the situation. In 2009, the first National Skill Development Policy was formed. Subsequently a National skill Development Mission was launched. Under the Mission, skill training of the heterogeneous labour consisting of youth, women, school dropouts, disabled, minorities, tribal groups were mandated.

Skill development was one of the priority agendas of the government for the 12th Five Year Plan. The government planned sector skill councils to complement the existing vocational education system for the industry in meeting the entire value chain's requirements of appropriately trained manpower in quantity and quality across all levels on a sustained and evolving basis.

Priority sectors identified in the 12th Five Year-Plan:

- Sector that will create large employment: Textile and garments, leather and footwear, gems and jewellery, food processing industries, handlooms and handicrafts.
- Sector that will deepen technology capabilities in manufacturing: Machine tools, IT hardware and electronics.

- Sector that will provide strategic security: Telecommunications equipment, aerospace, shipping, defense equipment.
- Manufacturing technology sectors for energy security: Solar energy, clean coal technologies, nuclear power generation.
- Capital equipment for India's infrastructure growth: Heavy electrical equipment, heavy transport, earth moving and mining equipment.
- Sectors where India has a competitive advantage: Automotive sectors, pharmaceutical and medical equipment.
- Micro, small and medium enterprises sector: The base for the manufacturing sector - employment and enterprise generation.

NDA Government's New Initiative

The NDA Government launched on 15th July 2015 Skill India Programme, a multi-skill programme. The main goal is to create opportunities, space and scope for the development of the talents of Indian youth and to develop more of those sectors which have already been put under skills development for the last many years and to identify new sectors for skill development. The new programme aims at providing training and skill development to 500 million youth of our country by 2022 covering each and every village and town.

Features of Skill India Programme

- The emphasis is to skill the youths in such a way so that they get employment and also improve entrepreneurship
- Provides training support and guidance for all occupations that are of traditional type like carpenters.
- More emphasis will be given on new areas like real estate, construction, transportation, textile, gem industry, jewellery designing, banking, tourism and various other sectors, where skill development is inadequate or till.
- The training programmes would be on the lines of international level so that the youths of our country can not only meet the domestic demands but also of other countries like the US, Japan, China, Germany, Russia and those in the West Asia.
- Another remarkable feature of the 'Skill India' programme would be to create a hallmark called 'Rural India Skill', so as to standardize and certify the training process.

- Tailor-made, need-based programmes would be initiated for specific age groups which can be like language and communication skills, life and positive thinking skills, personality development skills, management skills, behavioral skills, including jobs and employability skills.
- The course methodology of 'Skill India' would be innovative, which would include games discussions brainstorming sessions, practical experiences, case studies etc.

Various Initiatives under Skill India Programme

- National Skill Development Mission
- National Policy for Skill Development and Entrepreneurship, 2015
- Pradhan Mantri Kaushal Vikas Yojana (PMKVY)
- Rural India Skill

India's first Department of Skill Development and Entrepreneurship was established in July 2014 under the Ministry of Youth Affairs and Sports to specifically focus on addressing the above challenges. This Department became a full-fledged Ministry of Skill Development and Entrepreneurship (MSDE) in November 2014. The primary focus of MSDE is to develop a robust policy framework and programme of action for scaling up skill development efforts in India.

MSDE has taken three major policy initiatives during its first few months of existence.

National Policy for Skill Development and Entrepreneurship 2015, unveiled in July 2015. The policy articulates a framework for skilling at scale and speed while ensuring high quality outcomes. Policy implementation unit (PIU) set up and a system of quarterly monitoring of key elements of policy has been established.

National Skill Development Mission approved in July 2015. The Mission seeks to converge, coordinate, implement and monitor skilling activities on a pan-India basis. Governing Council, Steering Committee and Exceptive Committee notified. Sub Missions and interface with State Skill Missions would be made operational within March'16.

Common Norms for all skill development programmes across Central Ministries/Departments have been notified. Meeting and consultations for adoption of Common Norms held. Complete alignment to be done by 1.4.2016.

India now has a robust policy framework to scale up skill development initiatives across the country. Having set out the policy framework, MSDE has also been working on developing a coherent programme of action.

Central Ministries/ Departments Signing MoUs with Ministry of Skill Development and Entrepreneurship for Skill Development

1. Department of Empowerment of Persons with Disabilities
2. Ministry of Defence
3. Ministry of Railways
4. Ministry of Health & Family Welfare
5. Dept. of Fertilisers
6. Dept. of Chemicals and Petro-Chemicals
7. Dept. of Pharmaceuticals
8. Ministry of Steel
9. Ministry of Mines
10. Coal India (Ministry of Coal)
11. National Thermal Power Corporation, Power Grid (Ministry of Power)
12. Department of Heavy Industries
13. Ministry of Overseas Indian Affairs
14. Airport Authority of India

Overall Key Elements of MoUs

- Leverage existing government infrastructure to deliver skill programmes
- Mobilize CSR funds of Public Sector Undertaking (PSUs) to support skilling
- Upgrade equipment of ITIs and NSDC/SSC affiliated training providers
- Promote and scale up apprenticeship training in PSUs in coordination with DGT
- Incentivize hiring of NSQF certified personnel
- Promote adoption of ITIs by PSUs, including provision of technical and resource support
- Introduce vocational courses in schools run by Ministries/PSUs
- Establish 'Centres of Excellence' for high quality skill training
- Align training programmes to NSQF and mobilize workforce for Recognition of Prior Learning (RPL)

Out of all the achievements of Ministry of Skill Development and Entrepreneurship, the key achievements can be notified as:

- More than 1.17 crore people trained under MSDE programs
- 26.5 Lakhs candidates trained under MSDE's flagship scheme Pradhan Mantri Kushal Vikas Yojana
- More than 4.82 lakh people were brought into the organized sector through the recognition of prior learning program under PMKVY which recognises existing skills and certifies youth (13000 Rubber Tappers. More than 250 Railway Porters and 1500 Employees of Rashtrapati Bhawan)
- More than 480 Pradhan Mantri Kushal Kendras have been announced which would be in each district of the country for skilling and would be in each district of the country for ease of skilling. 162 are already been established.
- More than 1381 new ITIs have been opened with more than 5 lakh seats and the entire ecosystem of it is have been reinvigorated and reenergized

The Way Ahead

Considering the magnitude of the challenge in terms of skilling about 15 million persons every year and ensuring that the workforce of 500 million is adequately skilled by 2022, it is required that the way forward comprises of adequate initiative to achieve these humungous target in the right 'scale' and 'speed'.

Some of the possible solutions to address the issues outlined by ICRA Management Consulting Services limits are:

1. *Targeting skill development at all levels of the 'skill pyramid':* it is required to not only skill and educates the workforce at the higher skill levels (which is key to ensuring industry competitiveness through research and IP, etc). but also to adequately skill the workforce at the lower levels (i.e. where much of the workforce is concentrated).

   Accordingly, it is required that skill development initiatives be targeted at all levels of the 'skill pyramid'.
2. *Implementing Vocational Education in Schools:* Vocational Education in schools should be enhanced. This will present a channel for students to acquire skills, both life skills and industry-specific skills during schooling.

3. *Creating a large talent pool through Modular Employable Skills:* The MES framework provides a means for multiple-entry and multiple-exit skill development. It brings with it a flexibility to offer short-term, demand-led courses with partnership. Increased adoption and will help achieve the required scale in skill development.
4. *Ensuring Quality in Delivery:* Quality will have to be driven (as well as be determined) by the following dimensions at the level of each/individual institute/centre:

    - Strong Government and Administration
    - Adequate and appropriate faculty
    - Current curriculum
    - Relevant infrastructure
    - A defined process for evaluation of student learning from in-gate to out-gate, employment, and employability
    - Rewarding partnerships.

5. *Employing technology to achieve scale:* Information and Communication Technology (ICT)- led interventions will help achieve scaleability, standardization and maximization of impact.
6. *Formulation of institutional mechanism for content formation, delivery, and assessment:* At the demand for training grows, there will be also be a cascading impact on the demand for content, standardized processes for training delivery, uniform assessment practices. These will drive the demand for trainers and assessors which will be a critical bottleneck as other pieces of the ecosystem fall in place. Furthermore, there would be a need for standards and quality processes (quality system, formulation, quality assessment, quality certification training process certification) as the demand for training grows rapidly. These would require institutional mechanisms, specifying quality standards and practices.
7. *Expending the formulation of Sector Skill Councils:* Given the need to ensure standards, industry involvement and industry led initiatives, it is required to expedite the formulation of Sector Skill Councils.
8. *Setting up a National Human Resource Market Information System (a National Skill Exchange):* The requirement for an ICT-enabled market information system will help both employers and employees provide details on specific demand, as where the access to the skilled workforce exits. This should not only be limited to the vocationally skilled workforce but also be made available on the higher skill levels as well.

It is hoped that the above issues will help in transforming the skill development landscape in India as well as in improving and aiding the implementation of quality in skills training.

2

Skill Development Ecosystem

The skill development ecosystem in India is complex, large and diverse, providing varied levels of skills across an extremely heterogeneous population. Skill development in India can be broadly segmented into Education and Vocational training. The figure below presents the broads frameworks of skill development in India.

Elementary, secondary and higher education is governed by the Ministry of Human Resource Development. University and Higher Education caters to all college education (Arts, Science, Commerce, etc), while engineering education, polytechnics, etc, fall under Technical Education. University Grants Commission (UGC) is the nodal body governing funds, grants and setting standards for teaching, examination and research in Universities, and the All India Council for Technical Education (AICTE) is the regulatory body for Technical Education in India.

Skills in India are acquired through both formal and informal channels. Formal vocational training is imparted in both public and private sectors. Some of the major channels of formal vocation training include the government-run Industrial Training Institutes (ITIs), privately operated Industrial Training Centres (ITCs), vocational schools, specialized institutes for technical training and apprenticeship training by the industry. The private sector participation has been on a rise lately, but the sector continues to be dominated by the public sector. Informal training on the other hand refers to experiential skills acquired on the job.

At the central level, the nodal institution for vocational training is the Director General of Employment & Training (DGET) under the Ministry of Labour and Employment. The DGET is responsible for

India's Education and Skill Development Structure

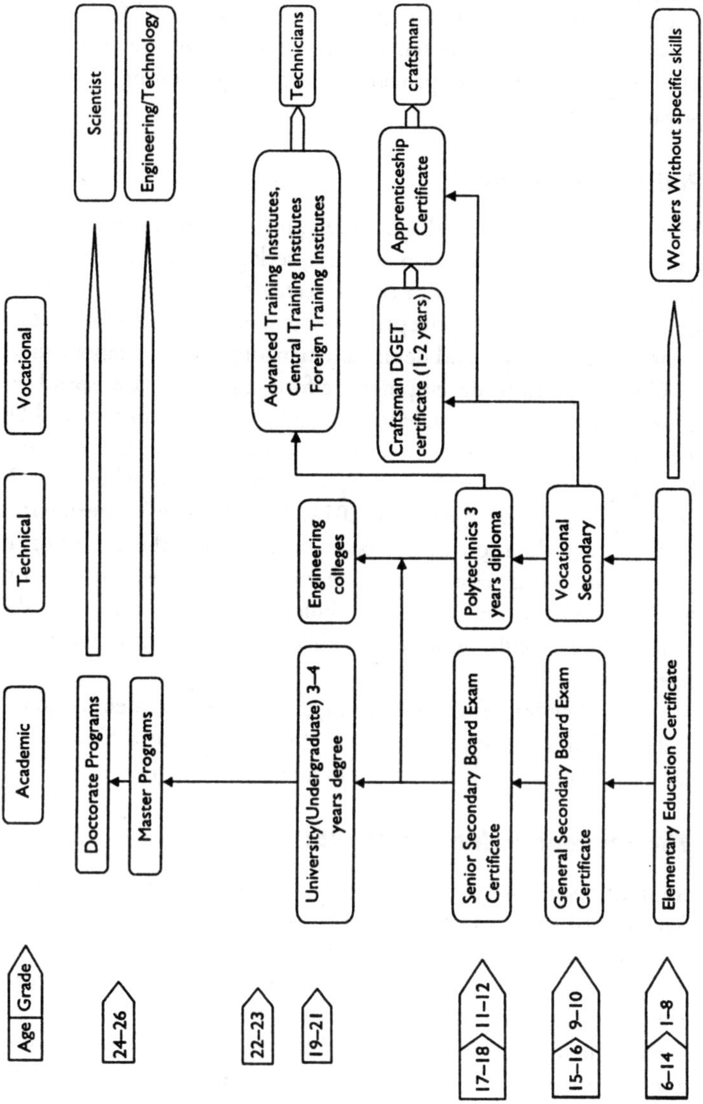

formulating policies, establishing standards, granting affiliation, trade testing and certification, and matters connected to vocational training and providing employment services. The National Skill Development Council (NSDC) – now a part of the newly created Ministry of Skill Development and Entrepreneurship – was initially set up under the Ministry of Finance to provide viability gap funding and promote private skill initiatives.

Policy Framework

The government has listed skill development as one of its priorities and aims to enhance participation of youth, seek greater inclusion of women, disabled and other disadvantaged sections into the workforce, and improve the capability of the present system, making it flexible to adapt to technological changes and demands emanating from the labour market.

Currently, skill development efforts in India are spead across approximately 20 separate Ministries, 35 State Government and Union Territories and the private sector. A Ministry of Skills Development, Entrepreneurship, Youth and Sports was created when the Modi government took charge in mid-2014. The Ministry has been entrusted with the coordination of all stakeholders during the evolution of an appropriate skills development framework, removal of disconnect between demand and supply of skilled manpower, skill upgradation, building new skills, innovative thinking and assuring availability of talents.

The policy framework governing the skill development ecosystem in India includes the Apprentices Act, 1961, the National Skill Policy and the National Skills Qualification Framework (NSQF).

The Apprenticeship Act of 1961

Apprenticeship programmes in India are governed by The Apprentice Act of 1961 and the Apprenticeship Rules of 1992. The organization structure and rules and regulations overseeing it are complex and burdensome. The Apprentice Training Scheme is implemented by the Ministries of Labour and Employment and Human Resource Development. The Ministry of Labour and Employment oversees 'trade apprentices' through six regional offices. The Ministry of Human resource Development oversees 'graduate, technician, and technician (vocational) apprentices' through four boards located in different cities.

The ACT regulates programmes of training of apprentices and makes it obligatory for employers in both public and private sector establishments to have training infrastructure as detailed in the Act. This has been primarily to ensure trainees get optimum access to real work environment and on-the-job training. One of the objectives of apprenticeship was also to ensure that employers get skilled workforce having adequate exposure to real work environment. About 254 groups of industries are covered under the Act and about 27,000 establishments engage apprentices.

However, there has not been much success in implementation of this Act. Although Apprenticeship Training Scheme has been running for over four decades, there has not been any significant improvement in respect of seat location as well utilization. The key issues with the apprentices system in India relate to low participation of workers and employers, low rates of stipend, strict regulatory requirements for employers including penalties for non-compliance, less coverage of trades in services sector and lack of progression into higher qualifications.

The Apprentice Act of 1961 was recently amended in December 2014 to make it more responsive to industry and youth. The Apprentice Protsahan yojana was also launched to support MSMEs in the manufacturing sector in engaging apprentices. As per the amended Act, work hours and leave benefits of Apprentices will be at par with the regular workers from the organized sector. Industries will be allowed to take more non-engineer graduates and diploma holders as apprentices, depending on the nature of the job, and new trades for apprenticeship training will be introduced. A portal is also being setup to make all approvals transparent and time bound.

The National Skill Policy

The National Policy on skill Development was first formulated in 2009 to create a skills ecosystem in India. It acts as a guide to formulate strategies by addressing the different challenges in skill development. The objective is to empower the workforce with the required skills, knowledge and qualifications to make the Indian workforce globally competitive.

The Government has introduced National Policy on Skill Development and Entrepreneurship, 2015. The policy aims to provide an umbrella framework to all skill related activities carried out within the country, to align them to common standards and link skill activities with demand centres. In addition to laying down the objectives and expected outcomes, it aims at identifying various institutional frameworks which can act as the vehicle to reach the expected outcomes. The new skills policy also provides details on how skill development efforts across the country can be aligned within the existing institutional arrangements.

The National Skills Qualification Framework

The National Skills Qualifications Framework (NSQF), notified on 27th December 2013, ia a competency-based framework that organizes all qualifications according to a series of levels of knowledge, skills and attitude. Presently, more than 100 countries have, or are in the process of developing national qualification frameworks.

Under NSQF, the learner can acquire the certification for competency needed at any level through formal, non-formal or informal learning. The NSQF is anchored at the National Skill Development Agency (NSDA) and is being implemented through the National Skills Qualifications Committee (NSQC) which comprises of all key stakeholders.

Specific outcomes expected from implementation of NSQF are:

- Mobility between vocational and general education by harmonization of degrees with NSQF;
- Recognition of Prior Learning (RPL), allowing transition from non-formal to organized job market;
- Standardized, consistent, nationally acceptable outcomes of training across the country through a national quality assurance framework;
- Global mobility of skilled workforce from India, through international equivalence of NSQF;
- Mapping of progression pathways within sectors and cross-sectorally;
- Approval of National Occupational Standards (NOS)/ Qualification Packs (QPs) as national standards for skill training;

As of 31st March 2015, across 28 sectors, standards for 1319 job roles pegged at NSQF levels 1 to 8 have been defined by the Sector Skill Councils (SSCs). Fourteen SSCs have covered development of 80 per cent of entry level workforce QPs.

The NSQF provides for a five year implementation schedule and at the end of the fifth year (2018), it shall be mandatory for all training/ educational programmes/courses to be NSQF-complaint, and all training and educational institutions shall define eligibility criteria for admission to various courses in terms of NSQF levels.

The system of multi-entry and multi-exit will enable students to acquire some skills after finishing compulsory general schooling, then enter the labour market and gain some work experience and return to the vocational education and training system to continue their vocational education/training. It would be particularly beneficial for relatively poor students, since it would enable them to continue in either the vocational stream of the secondary system or the ITI system, rather than dropping out from the educational or vocational training space altogether.

Nodal Bodies for Skill Development in India

Ministry of Skill Development in India

The creation of the first-ever separate Ministry of Skill Development and Entrepreneurship was announced by Prime Minister Narendea Modi in June 2014. It is conceived to encompass all other ministries to work in a unified way, set common standards, as well as coordinate and streamline the functioning of different organizations working for skill development.

The Ministry of Skill Development and Entrepreneurship is entrusted to make broad policies for all other ministries' skill development initiatives and National Skill Development Corporation (NCDC). Mapping and certifying skills, market research and designing curriculum, encouraging education in entrepreneurship, make policies for boosting soft skills and computer education to bridge the demand and supply gaps are among the others goals.

MHRD

The Ministry of Human Resource and Development (MHRD) governs the polytechnic institutions offering diploma level courses under various disciplines such as engineering and technology, pharmacy, architecture, applied arts and crafts and hotel management. MHRD is also involved in the scheme of Apprenticeship Training, Apart from this, MHRD has also introduced vocational education from class IX onwards, and provides financial assistance for engaging with industry/ SSCs for certification and training.

Central Ministries

There are 21 Ministries under the central government who are also working for the purpose of skill development. There are two approaches that these Ministries have: one approach is setting up training centres of their own for specific sectors like (adopted by Ministry of Labour & Employment, Ministry of Agriculture, Ministry of Health & Family Welfare, etc). The second approach is in the form of Public Private Partnership (as adopted by Ministry of Rural Development, Ministry of Women and Child Development, etc).

Enabling Agencies

NSDC

The National Skill Development Corporation India (NSDC) is a public private partnership organization (now under the Ministry of Skill Development and Entrepreneurship) that was incorporated in 2009 under the National Skill Policy. Its main aim is to provide viability gap funding to private sector in order to scale up training capacity.

The NSDC has tied up with more than 187 training providers, many of whom have started scaling up their operations.

The NSDC has also been entrusted to set up SSCs ensuring right representation of employers and to extend financial support to operationalise them. It also undertakes research initiatives, pilot projects, and skill gap studies to create a knowledge base for the sector. They have supported and incubated 31 SSCs that is intended to facilitate the much needed participation and ownership of the industry to ensure needs-based training programmes.

The National Skill Development Agency (NSDA) is working with the State governments to rejuvenate and synergise skilling effort in the State. The National Skills Qualification Framework (NSQF) has been anchored at NSDA and efforts have been initiated to align all skilling and education outcomes with the competency based NSQF levels.

The NSDCs mandate also involves capacity building by working with different stakeholders and identifying best practices to create an excellence model. The NSDC has also been working to create awareness about the skill ecosystem and has rolled out electronic and print campaigns.

Sector Skill Councils

The National Skill Development Policy of 2009 mandated the NSDC to setup SSCs to bring together key stakeholders i.e. industry, work force and academic. They are funded by NSDC for the initial few years and are expected to become financially self-sustaining as they grow.

These SSCs are expected to lay down the National Occupational Standards for different levels of jobs in their respective sectors, formulate certification and accreditation norms, strive to create knowledge repository on current requirement of skill development in the industry, assess the supply of skilled workers, identify the demand and supply gap in each sector, and identify trends and future requirements. With availability of trainers being a major challenge in scaling up the capacity, SSCs are also expected to play a crucial role in getting right industry support to facilitate training of trainers for their respective sectors.

NCVT, SCVT and Quality Council of India

Established under Ministry of Labour and Employment with with a view to ensure and maintain uniformity in the standards of training all over the country, the National Council for Vocational Training (NCVT) was set up in 1956. This certifying body conducts All India Trade Tests for those who complete training in ITIs and awards National Trade Certificates to successful candidates. The Council has representation from central and state government departments, employers' and workers' organizations, professional and learned bodies, All India Council for Technical Education, scheduled castes and scheduled tribes, All India Women's Organisation, among other. The State Council for Vocational Training at the State levels and the sub committees have been established to assist National Council.

The Quality Council of India (QCT) was set up jointly by Government of India and the Indian industry as an autonomous body to establish a national accreditation structure in the field of education, healthcare, environment protection, governance, social sectors, infrastructure, vocational training and other areas that have significant bearing in improving the quality of life. All institutions (Government and private ITIs) seeking formal affiliation from NCVT have to first get accreditation from the Quality Council of India.

Implementing Agencies

Industrial Training Institutes

The DGET which governs Industrial Training Institutions (ITIs) has recently been aligned with Ministry of Skill Development and Entrepreneurship. There are more than 10,000 ITIs with a capacity of approximately 1.5 million seats. The DGET also govern RVITs (Regional Vocational Training Institutions) and ATIs (Advance Training Institutions) focusing on specialized and high-end skill sets and trainers courses.

These majour skill development schemes of the DGET that are being implemented through government ITIs and private ITCs include the Craftmen Training Scheme, the Apprenticeship Training Scheme, and the Modular Employability Scheme.

- Craftmen Training Scheme: the scheme is being run in over 10,000 institutes with a seating capacity of about 1.3 million. The training is available for about 116 trades and the course generally has duration of 2 years. The courses generally require a minimum education qualification of having passed the 10th or 12th grade (some trades accepts students who have passed the 8th grade). Under these schemes, emphasis is largely on the practical aspects, with practical to theory teaching ratio being 70:30.
- Apprenticeship Training Scheme: As mentioned earlier, around 27,000 establishments are providing apprenticeship training to 211,632 youths (for 2013-14). The training usually varies between 6 months to 4 years. The minimum educational qualification is different for different trades. For some trades, educational qualification is SSC passed or equilent, whereas for some it is two classes below SSC.
- Modular Employability Skills: the programme was initiated in 2007 with the objective of expanding the outreach of the training facilities to school dropouts and in recognition of need for prior learning of worker in the unorganized sector. The target workers include those who have left school after 5th or 6th grade or have acquired on-job-training but do not have formal certification. Under this scheme, short duration courses are provided to prospective trainees using both government and private infrastructure. 1,402 modules covering more than 60

sectors have been developed, 36 Assessing Bodies empanelled for conducting assessment, 6,951 Vocational Training Providers (VTPs) registered and more than 1.35 million persons have been trained/tested up to 31-3-2012.

Private Training Service Providers

The private sector has been taking various initiatives on its own and in collaboration with the government and international entities, to upgrade in-house training facilities and also to provide training to potential employees to make them job-ready.

Many large corporation like Larsen & Toubro, Bharti Groups, Hero Groups, Maruti, ITC, Infrastructure Leasing & Finance Service Ltd etc, have established training facilities that offer world-class training programmes. The government provides partial support in funding by way of sponsoring the tuition fee of the students.

NSDC has 203 training partners under its PPP module, which include for-profit as well as non-profit entities. In the last four years, these training partners have trained over 2 million people in more than 25 sectors at 2500+ fixed and mobile centres in over 350 districts across the country.

3

Need to Re-engineer Skill Ecosystem

India symbolises a remarkable growth story for the world and Skill India is one of Prime Minister Narendra Modi's flagship initiatives, aimed at sustaining this growth story and making India the world economic leader. In fact, predicted to grow at 7.5 per cent — 7.7 per cent per annum, India is expected to sustain its position as the world's fastest growing economy till 2018.

A forecast by the Ministry of Skill Development and Entrepreneurship (MSDE) suggests there would be an incremental requirement of skilling 110 million additional workers by 2022. It is obvious that India will have to rethink its skilling capacities for the existing and future workforce in order to achieve this.

Delving deeper into the issue, FICCI and KPMG in India together launched a white paper titled 'Re-engineering the skill ecosystem'. The report examines the complexity and diversity of the country in terms of economic development, demography, geography, internal and international migration and unavailability of relevant data, and recommends the way forward.

As per the report, an interesting characteristic of the employment growth story has been the growth in the formal workforce. The estimation of the number of employees in various social security benefit schemes indicates that nearly 114 million employees or 22 per cent (2014–15) are in formal employment. This number has been steadily rising. The report suggests two important trends, vis-à-vis the Indian workforce that call for attention and action— first, the scope of job creation in formal employment opportunities and second, the implications of Industry 4.0 on future jobs.

The report states that the future Indian consumer will reside in Tier 2 and Tier 3 cities. Hence, predictably, this market is likely to be the centre of attraction for global and Indian consumer focussed industries. The services and manufacturing sectors are likely to create more employment opportunities. With government schemes like Make in India, eased out FDI companies like Apple, Xiaomi, LeEco, Suzuki and others from across the globe are seeing great investment opportunities in India.

However, this also means the country will have to gear up to meet the demand for skilled workforce generated from these foreign investments. Undoubtedly, to reach the full potential, India will have to gravitate towards a formal system. To accomplish this and reskill the existing workforce, MSDE has already embarked on a herculean task of skilling 400 million by 2022. Mohandas Pai, chairman FICCI Skill Development Committee and chairman Manipal Global Education, says, "There is an urgent need to evaluate our current scenario, look at future projections and re-engineer the skill ecosystem accordingly."

The issues that form roadblocks in our current skilling framework are few yet complicated. First, the women Worker Population Ratio (WPR) in India is about one-third that of the male WPR. According to data from the World Bank, India ranks 10th from the bottom, globally, in terms of women labour participation. The other two important issues that emerge upon analysing the rising number of unemployed graduates are — poor quality of education and a mismatch in the demand and supply of education or skills. The low women WPR requires policy action combined with conscious efforts by the private sector to reduce impediments to equal access to jobs. Improvement in the quality of education needs government action to develop an integrated and dynamic educational system.

Also, in the larger context of growing formal employment and industry, it becomes more critical to focus on integrating the education system to meet new skill needs in a timely manner. The challenge for skill India is that education and skill training are delivered in parallel, in a siloed manner. Formal education is delivered through traditional universities and polytechnics. Industrial Training Institutions (ITI) act as primary institutions to deliver skill training, focusing mostly on technical trades. However, these systems operate in silos with limited options for vertical and horizontal mobility. Additionally, especially with regard to skill training, unlike the US, UK or Australia the critical component of industry linkage is missing in the Indian ecosystem.

The renowned German dual system, for example, offers well-integrated vocational training programmes that begin at the school level. A key differentiating factor that drives quality of education is the strong apprenticeship-linkage during training, where a student opting for vocational education, spends approximately three and a half days per week getting on-the-job training and the rest at the vocational school. At the same time, vocational education systems in Australia and the UK are clear examples of the excellent coordination between the industry and the vocational programme, wherein the industry is involved at each stage from the curriculum design to its validation.

Shobha Mishra Ghosh, senior director-FICCI adds, "Vocational education and skill development have never been aspirational in our country. In India, 77 per cent of those above 30 years and 42 per cent in the age group 18–29 years are employed. There is an urgent need to integrate skill development within our formal education to meet the 21st century skill requirements."

Taking cues from the examples, the report suggests that the Indian government formulate a system, which ensures a regular feedback mechanism from the industry whilst designing and updating the Technical Vocational Education and Training (TVET) courses. This would go a long way in propelling the advent of vocational education and create its acceptability among the wider masses. Narayanan Ramaswamy, partner and head, education and skill development, KPMG in India, says, "The bright side to the challenge of skill development is that the government recognises India's favourable demographic dividend and is shouldering the responsibility of providing employment to the millions of youth in a big way. However, nothing short of a revolution is required in the skilling and vocational education space, which in my view has assumed critical proportions and might well determine the future growth of this country."

In order to provide the right opportunities for skill training to ensure timely availability of skilled manpower, the FICCI–KPMG white paper recommends the following strategic changes to re-engineer the ecosystem that can facilitate the transformation.

Policy-level actions: Developing skill development plans based on state-level analyses, of the major industries driving economic growth and rising formal employment opportunities by state and central governments, is essential. With future growth coming from formal employment, an intensive recognition of prior learning exercise to certify available skills as per the National Skills Qualification Framework level also becomes vital.

Quality enhancement actions: An active role of industry is key to improving the aspirational value of skill training programmes in India. Upgrading existing skillsets of teachers also needs to be formally undertaken. Special incentives can be provided to the industry by the government in order to invest their two per cent CSR funds towards skilling initiatives in order to ensure adequate capitalisation.

Other systematic improvements: Improving the WPR of women through women-centric component in Skill State Plans and annually monitoring and recognising high-performing states could be a positive step in this direction. Establishing and growing more skill universities is also one of the key suggestions.

It is now evident that to fulfill the future requirement for skilled talent and to make the most of the growth opportunities, all the stakeholders — the government, industry, training partners, learners and other service providers need to work alongside to create a robust and resilient skilling ecosystem. This will not only ensure long-term sustainability of the skilling system but will also help in changing the perception of the labour populace in general, towards skilling.

4

Skills Structure

Governance: Union and State Responsibilities

As a federal country, the Constitution of India defines the distribution of responsibilities for key policy areas by creating three lists.

In the Skills Sector, there is a mix of Central Schemes, designed and funded centrally, with some front line support from the states. Two significant central schemes are Pradhan Mantri Kaushal Vikas Yojana (PMKVY) under the Ministry of Skills Development and Entrepreneurship, and Deen Dayal Upadhyaya Grameen Kaushalya Yojana (DDU-GKY) under the Ministry of Rural Development. Both schemes engage private training providers to create courses development by Sector Skills Councils. These courses are based on National Occupational Standards (NOS) and Qualification Packs (QPs).

Two examples of state-level responsibilities are the management of Industrial Training Institutes (ITIs), which impart skill training to students, and the State Skill Development Missions, which are responsible for integrating various skill development efforts within the states.

Board Classification of Delivery Agents for Skill Development

There are five major pillars for skills training in India.

- Directorate General for Training
- NSDC affiliated organizations
- AICTE affiliated organizations
- Senior secondary schools
- Private unaided training providers

The fifth pillar-the private unaided training sector, as in all countries, is probably the largest and hardest to quantify. It is not reliant on any source of public funding and is largely unregulated and unmapped.

An overview of training providers and certification bodies which are common to all five pillars. Then have a look at groups of organizations that are unique to one or more pillars, including capacity building organizations, assessment bodies and apprenticeship boards.

Training Organisations

As in all sectors of education, there are three broad groups of training providers.

- Government managed and funded organizations;
- Privately managed and government funded (aided) organization; and
- Privately funded and managed organizations.

Industrial Training Institutes (ITIs)

These are the most numerous of the dedicated TVET institutions. They formally started in the late 1960s and are funded at a state level. These institutions generally provide the Craftsmen Training scheme (CTS), which is certificated by the National Council for Vocational Training (NCVT). The CTS scheme is made up of 12 year courses, depending on the trade and generally targets students who have passed 12th standard (A-levels) or 10th standard (GCSEs), depending on the trade. CTS has great brand visibility among employers, learners and parents, through there is concern about how up to date the courses are from an industry perspective. The ability to innovative curriculum in order to respond to employer demands is limited by formal theoretical assessments and by the lack of modern infrastructure and equipments.

ITIs are also able to deliver short course skills training through the Skill Development Initiative Modular Employability Scheme (SDI MES), which is also certified by the NCVT. There is a greater diversity of courses under this scheme and is more responsive to industry needs though the depth of training is limited compared to the CTS.

SDI MES was initiated in 2009 and there are 91 sectors in which courses are currently available. Convergence through the NSQF may also upgrade these courses to align to industry standards. SDI MES courses, alongside courses developed by SSCs, are generally the two certification schemes preferred by the state skill Development Missions.

Government-run ITIs are generally larger and run a number of trades, as well as SDI MES courses. There are approximately 126 trades offered through CTS can broken down as follows:

- 73 engineering courses like diploma in Chemical Engineering. Civil Engineering and Instrumentation & control
- 48 non-engineering courses like M.Sc, BBA and MCA
- 5 courses exclusively for the visually impaired such as courses in metal cutting attendant.

The largest of ITIs cater to around 2000 students. Compared to UK colleges, they are relatively small and to engage with them individually from an international perspective would pose a challenge. Teacher training and capacity building for ITIs is supported by a network of central and state-level institutions (more details given below), which would provide a more strategic platform for engagement. Such an engagement would be best initiated through the Central or State Government.

Polytechnics form the next largest group of institutions. These institutions target higher level skills and are generally considered to be part of the higher education sector. They are funded and regulated by the all India Council of Technical Education (AICTE) and supervised at the state level by the Directorate of Technical Education. Polytechnics, including specialist institutions such as Nursing Colleges or dedicated institutions for women, are a mix of public and private institutions. They offer three-year Diploma programmes on a wide range of technical subjects, from bio-technology to jewellery designing.

Certification Bodies

India has recently introduced the National Skills Qualification Framework (NSQF). The framework will unify the norms for certification for all government-funded training programmes delivered by public and private training bodies. Three types of organizations currently provide certificates for these schemes:

- National Council for Vocational Training (NCVT) (awards National Trades Certificates)
- All India Council for Technical Education (AICTE) (awards Diplomas)
- Sector Skill Council (awards Sector Specific Certificates)

The first two organizations are national certification boards that cover multiple subjects. Sector Skills Councils are sector specific. In the 2016 Budget announcement a new National Board for Skill Development Certification has been proposed, which is likely to unify the certification currently issued by NCVT and Sector Skills Councils.

As in the UK, there is a regulatory framework for privately-funded certification. As such, the variety of certification is limitless and includes professional and language Qualifications. There are a number of high profile national and international certificates, which rely on brand and reputation for currency, with a high visibility in India. A number of international certificates have been integrated into programmes offered by the traditional TVET institutions and universities through the alignment of curriculum and a separate fee paid directly by the student. In the technical sector, CISCO is a good example of an international certificate that falls into this category. In the higher education space, the Association of Chartered Certified Accountants (ACCA) is a common example.

Capacity Building

Traditional TVET institutions and schools are supported through a network of capacity building institutions that support curriculum development and faculty training. The institutions generally align to the certifying body.

For NCVT certified courses, there is a network of 30 central institutes. The most prominent institution in this sector is the Central Staff Training & Research Institute (CSTARI) in Kolkata, through there are a number of Advanced Training Institutes (ATIs) and increasing state level faculty training institutes to provide greater access to training.

Support is provided to school through the Pandit Sunderlal Sharma Central Institute of Vocational Education (PSSCIVE), which is a specialist institution in the National Council of Educational Research and Training (NCERT). The organization recently developed a NSQF Cell, which supports the introduction of competence-based qualifications in schools that work closely with SSCs. The NSQF Cells provides advice to the Ministry of Human Resource Development (MHRD) and supports the development of curriculum and faculty training.

In addition to certificates, Sector Skills Council is responsible for developing the National Occupation Standards (NOS) that represent industry norms for competence as well as Qualification Packs (QP) that bring these together into a coherent training programme. SSCs also provide faculty training for their affiliated partners

Assessment Bodies

Assessment Bodies are relatively unique in India. A significant percentage of assessments for the National Boards (NCVT and AICTE) are delivered by them through state-level government agencies, However, with the introduction of the SDI-MES scheme in 2009, additional capacity was required to deliver assessments for the increased number of short courses. Assessment bodies are private assessment agencies that will often have existing business in the privately-funded training sector. In order to assess under the SDI-MES, suitably qualified bodies had to be recognized by the NCVT. As SSCs started to establish and issued their first NOS and QPs, a similar exercise was undertaken to deliver assessment through suitably qualified assessment bodies.

Apprenticeships

Apprenticeships are defined under the original Apprenticeships Act in 1961. This act has been amended a number of times, most recently in 2014. Two parallel schemes operate under the principle ministries. Trade apprentices are governed by the Apprenticeship Training Scheme, under the Directorate of Training and implemented through six Regional Directorates of Apprenticeships Training (RDATs) located at Kolkata, Mumbai, Chennai, Hyderabad, Kanpur and Faridabad. Higher Level Apprenticeships are the responsibility of the Ministry of Human Resource Development and are implemented by four regional Boards of Apprenticeship Training (BOAD) (Mumbai, Chennai, Kanpur and Kolkata).

Unlike the Apprenticeships system in the UK, the costs of the scheme are born wholly by the employer, including training costs. The development and delivery of training is driven primarily by the employer in line with legislation. Though this approach fragments the delivery of the scheme, it is needed because apprenticeship must be very closely aligned to employers' specific needs. Recent significant changes have been made to the Apprenticeship Training Scheme (ATS) that can benefit UK companies based in India. The most notable is the National Apprenticeship Promotion Scheme, under which 25 per cent of the stipend for apprentices will be reimbursed to the firm hiring apprentices. This initiative seeks to scale up apprenticeships training. This along with the recent amendments to the Apprentices Act could play an important role in scaling up apprenticeship training.

Industry Bodies

Industry bodies play a unique and extensive role in the Skills sector in India. Not only do they represent Industry from a policy perspective, but they also play active part in the Skills sector. The three main industry bodies that are most active in the Skills sector are the Confederation of Indian Industries (CII), Federation of Indian Chambers of Commerce & Industry (FICCI) and The Associated Chambers of Commerce & Industry of India (ASSOCHAM).

All three are involved in research in the sector and the first two hold National Annual events that bring together industry. Training provides and Government officials. All three also play an active role in the delivery of skills training, which includes housing Sector Skills Councils, acting as an assessing bodies and direct training. More information on their specific activities in the skills sector can be found by following the link below:

- CII Skills
- FICCI Skill Development Forum
- ASSOCHAM Skill Development Centre

5

Skills Journey

It is not that skill and training have given high priority by the government for the first time under the current regime. Underlining the importance of skill development and vocational education, the 12th Five Year Plan (FYP) document informs us that while falling labour force is a major concern in most industrialized countries and also China, India has the benefit of a demographic dividend because the age structure of the population ensures that the labour force will be growing.

It is a different matter, however, that the Planning Commission, which prepared the plan was replaced by the NITI Aayog as soon as the NDA came to Power. Nevertheless, the importance of the 12th FYP document cannot be ignored.

The 12th FYP, which was prepared under the United Progressive Alliance in its second term (UPA-2), emphasizes the need to connect the Skill Development Mission with market demand. The document mentions that in order to ensure that skill match demand employers and enterprises must play a vital role to play in the conception and implementation of vocational training programmes, including managing Industrial Training Institutes (ITIs) and in the development of faculty.

The FYP document also calls for an enabling framework that would attract private investment in Vocational Training through Public-Private Partnership (PPP). The importance of harnessing the respective strengths of public and private sector entities engaged in skill development is underlined. Other areas of focus that the plan document spells out include mobilizing the required investments, setting up first rate ITIs, ensuring efficiency in operations and management and enabling post-training employment.

While these were considered the primary responsibilities of private sector entities, the government was also envisaged to play a role in providing an enabling framework and the requisite financial support, especially in respect of Scheduled Castes, Scheduled Tribes, minorities, differently-abled persons and other deprived sections of society.

The Plan says that skill development programmes should have backward linkages with school programmes and forward linkages with industry and other service sectors who can be potential employers of skilled manpower. It urges enhancing access to higher education by creating two million additional seats for each age cohort aligned to the skill needs of the economy.

In short, skill shortage was identified as a major constraint for attaining the growth of the manufacturing sector. It would, therefore, not be an exaggeration to say that the NDA is following in the footsteps of the previous UPA government for attaining higher growth by imparting skills to India's labour force

However, the 12th FYP embarked on a relative modest target of skilling 80 million people until 2019, which leaves around 400 million people to be trained in the 13th FYP by 2022, according to the 4th Annual Employment-Unemployment Survey Report 2013-14 of the Labour Bureau.

National Skill Development Policy (2009)

Despite the capacity of skill development programmes being just 3.1 million during 2009, the National Skill Development Policy (NSDP) of the UPA set a target of skilling 500 million people by 2022, which was a more higher target than that set under the Skill India Mission of the NDA.

Among other things, one of the operational strategies of the NSDP was to ensure availability of public institutions above the high school levels, which would offer training after class hours for skill development. The other strategy was to create a National Vocational Qualification Framework (NVQF) with an open/flexible system, which would permit individuals to acquire and build on their knowledge and skills, and convert them through testing and certification into higher diplomas and degrees.

The NSDP (2009) also addressed the need for strengthening the skill base of the unorganized sector so as to improve productivity, working condition, labour rights, social security and living standards.

National Skill Development Corporation (NSDC)

As per information accessed from its official website, the National Skill Development Corporation (NSDC) was set up as a not-for-profit public company under section 25 of the Companies Act 1956 in 2008 (under the UPA) with the approval of the Union Cabinet with the objective of increasing the skills training capacity in the country. It started with a capital base of Rs 10 crore, intended to encourage and synchronize private sector initiative in skills development.

The overall objective of the NSDC has been to create training capacity, fund scalability and sustainability of private enterprise, create a market ecosystem for skill development and meet the targets set out by the Government. The NSDC's mandate was to train 50 million people by 2022.

On whether the NSDC is monitored by the government, its website says that the Corporation submits data at regular intervals to the PM's National Council for Skill Development and subsequently to the National Skill Development Agency, as well as to the Ministry of Finance. Since the formation of the Ministry of Skill Development and Entrepreneurship, NSDC has sharing regular updates/information with the Ministries mutually agreed upon.

National Skill Development Agency (NSDA)

The National Skill Development Agency (NSDC) was notified through a gazette notification dated 6 June 2013 under the UPA. It is an autonomous body of the Ministry of Skill Development and Entrepreneurship which coordinates and harmonizes the skill development efforts of the Government and of the private sector, to achieve the skilling target of the 12th Plan.

It also endeavors to bridge the social, regional, gender and economic divide by ensuring that the skilling needs of the disadvantaged and marginalized groups are taken care of through the various skill development programmes and by taking various forms of affirmative action as part of advocacy by the NSDA.

As per information accessed from the NSDA website, nearly 2.79 crore people were trained between 2011-12 and October 2015-16. The site also informs us that the Government achieved 98.2 percent of its annual target in terms of training people in 2011-12, 72 percent in 2012-13, 104.01 percent in 2013-14, 72.43 percent in 2014-15 and 23.64 percent till October 2015-16. Going by this trend, there is no guarantee that the target of Skill India Mission of the NDA will be achieved.

National Skill Development Mission (NSDM)

The Union Cabinet chaired by Prime Minister Narender Modi on 2 July 2015 gave its approval for institutional framework for the NSDM, in keeping with the commitment made during the Budget Speech 2015-16. The NSDA, and the Directorate of Training were envisaged to work under the overall guidance of the Mission.

The Training and Apprenticeship verticals, comprised of the entire network of Industrial Training Institutes (ITIs) and Apprenticeship Training Schemes were transferred from the Ministry of Labour and Employment to the Ministry of Skill Development and Entrepreneurship (MSDE) on 16 April, 2015. In its press release dated 2 July 2015, the NDA government claims that these changes have paved the way for a new skilling ecosystem, with closer coordination across the public and private sectors.

However, as can be seen from the previous paragraphs pertaining to the 12th FYP, NSDP, NSDC and NSDA, the joint involvement of the private as well as the public sector in imparting skills to the labour force was emphasized even by the UPA government.

Narendra Modi launched the Skill India Mission on 15 July 2015. He also launched four landmark initiatives under the Ministry of Skill Development and Entrepreneurship, the National Skill Development Mission, National Policy for Skill Development and Entrepreneurship 2015, Pradhan Mantri Kaushal Vikas Yojana (PMKVY) scheme and the Skill Loan scheme.

Although a separate Ministry of Skill Development and Entrepreneurship has been created by the NDA Government for policy, coordination and capacity building through various related programmes, the Ministry has been allocated only Rs. 1543.46 crore in 2015-16 under the Union Budget, which comes to around Rs 12 per head.

6

National Skills Development Strategy

The National Skill Development mission, headed by the Prime Minister, was launched in 2008, and a Co-ordination Action Plan for Skill Development was formulated. A 3-tier structure has been created to take forward this plan. At its apex was the National Council on Skill Development, chaired by the Prime Minister and responsible for policy advice, direction and review. The core principles formulated by the Council were:

- Government money must target market failure: there is no need to crowd out or compete with private financing
- Decentralize: encourage and incentivize states to form skill missions
- Do not use money for building or hard assets
- Focus on modularity, open architecture, and short term courses: do not reimburse for courses more than six months
- Separate financing from delivery: make public money available for private and public delivery
- Link financing to outcomes: the overwhelming metric should be jobs
- Use candidates as financing vehicles rather than institutions: create choice and competition
- Create infrastructure for on job training: encourage apprenticeships
- Create Infrastructure for information asymmetry: publicize rating and outcome information for training institutions

- Infrastructure for effecting entry exit gate: effective assessments and credible certification
- Restructure employment exchanges to career centres

The second tire, the National Skill Development Co-ordination Board was chaired by the Deputy Chairman, Planning Commission. It expected to enumerate implementation strategies, formulating operational guidelines, and evaluating schemes. State Skill Development Boards were set up in states to address the specific problems of multiple interfaces with state government in getting approvals for central and state skill development schemes. The third tire is the National Skill Development Corporation (NSDC), set up as a non-profit company under the Companies Act, and mandated to support training initiatives. It had an equity base of Rs. 100 million, of which the private sector held 51 percent, while the Government of India controlled 49 percent. NSDC identified 20 high-growth, high-employment sectors (10 in manufacturing and 10 in services) for concentrated skill development to train 150 million people by 2022, with a special category added of the 'unorganized sector'. This was an important addition, as special effort needed to equip unorganized sector workers to access work in the growth sectors. Industry-led Sector Skill Councils (SSC) identified specific skill shortages and developed suitable training modules. Several SSCs were incorporated; others were approver by NSDC. The National Skill Development Fund was created by the Central Government to support these activities, and three of the first proposals to be accepted had come from diverse players: the Gems and Jewellery Export Promotion Council, Confederation of Indian Industry and the Self-Employed Women's Association.

At the base of the training systems, government run Industrial Training Institutes and private sector run Industrial Training Centres offered courses up to 24 months in different trades. A major criticism of these was limited employability due to curriculum rigidity and weak market responsiveness following upon poor industry-institution linkages. A World Bank tracer study conducted in 2006 showed that less than 30 percent ITI graduates found employment, and that employers wanted different technical skills and strong 'soft' skills: teamwork, innovativeness. Many new ITIs/ITCs offering certification in different trades were proposed to be set up.

The Skill Development Initiative Scheme of the Ministry of Labour and Employment started in 2007 focused on modular skills for employability, and roughly half of those trained, tested and certified under the scheme found employment by 2010.

The Ministry of Human Resource Development (MHRD), Government of India had proposed a National Vocational Education Qualifications Framework (NVEQF) which encouraged integration of vocational and general education. Suitable curricula were developed by the Central Board of Secondary Education. It proposed that school children would be involved in vocational education from Class 9. The NVEQF was expected set the principles for a nationally recognized qualification system, covering schools, vocational education institutes of higher education and for qualifications ranging from secondary school to doctorate level, leading to international recognition of national standards. The involvement of sector skill Councils and Industry in the development of standards and curricula would encourage linkage between education providers and employers. The transformation envisaged was profound, from 'an input based standards and supply led education system to an outcome based demand driven education and training system.

Responding to this environment, a new initiative started in 2010 was that of 'Community Colleges' where IGNOU (Indira Gandhi National Open University) in partnership with selected NGOs that conducted the courses, provided certification for those who were unable to access regular educational institutions. Community Colleges offered a 2 year curriculum that either led to an Associate Degree for transfer to an undergraduate college or to the students direct entry into any occupation or trade. Although a large number of NGOs responded to the call for partnership in 2010, little information was available on who participated, and whether the system was able to obtain study funding and adequate infrastructure, including attracting trained teachers into non-government system.

7

National Skill Development Mission

India currently faces a severe shortage of well-trained, skilled workers. It is estimated that only 2.3 per cent of the workforce in India has undergone formal skill training as compared to 68 per cent in the UK, 75 per cent in Germany, 52 per cent in USA, 80 per cent in Japan and 96 per cent in South Korea. Large sections of the educated workforce have little or no job skills, making them largely unemployable. Therefore, India must focus on scaling up skill training efforts to meet the demands of employers and drive economic growth. India's annual skilling capacity was estimated at approximately 7 million during the period 2013-2014. Apart from meeting its own demand, India has the potential to provide a skilled workforce to fill the expected shortfall in the ageing developed world. India is one of the youngest nations in the world, with more than 54 per cent of the total population below 25 years of age and over 62 per cent of the population in the working age group (15-59 years). The country's population pyramid is expected to bulge across the 15-59 age groups over the next decade. This demographic advantage is predicted to last only until 2040. India therefore has a very narrow time frame to harness its demographic divided and to overcome its skills shortages. The enormity of India's skilling challenge is further aggravated by the fact that skill training efforts cut across multiple sectors and require the involvement of diverse stakeholders such as: multiple government departments at the center and state levels, private training providers, educational and training institutions, employers, industry associations, and certification bodies and trainees. All this stakeholders need to align their work together in order to achieve the target of 'Skill India'.

The Ministry of Skill Development and Entrepreneurship (earlier Department of Skill Development and Entrepreneurship, first created in July 2014) was set up in November 2014 to drive the 'Skill India' agenda in a 'Mission Mode' in order to converge existing skill training initiatives and combine scale and quality of skilling efforts, with speed. The Ministry therefore, proposed to launched the National Skill Development Mission (NMSD –known henceforth as, the Mission), which will provide the overall institutional framework to rapidly implement and scale up skill development efforts across India. The vision, objectives and design of the Mission, draw on the lessons learnt from the implementation of skill development efforts over the past decade. It seeks to provide the institutional capacity to train minimum of 300 million skilled people by the year 2022. The Framework for implementation will provide strategic direction to state governments and establish a clear line of action to enable India to achieve its skilling targets. Effort is made here to outline the overall vision and objectives of the Mission. It then articulates the Mission's institutional structure (at the national, state and district level), outlines its strategy (by forcing on the launch of seven core sub-missions) and provides a brief on the financial model.

Mission Objectives

1. Create to end-to-end implantation framework, which provides opportunities for life-long learning. This includes: incorporation of skilling in the school curriculum, providing opportunities for quality long and short-term skill training, by providing gainful employment and ensuring career progression that meets the aspirations of trainees.
2. Align employers/industry demand and workforce productivity with trainees' aspirations for sustainable livelihoods, by creating a framework for outcome-focused training.
3. Establish and enforce cross-sectoral, nationally and internationally acceptable standards for skill training in the country by creating a sound quality assurance framework for skilling, applicable to all Ministries, States and private training providers.
4. Build capacity for skill development in critical un-organized sectors (such as the construction sector, where there few opportunities for skill training) and provide pathways for

re-skilling and up-skilling workers in these identified sectors, to enable them to transition into formal sector employment.

5. Ensure sufficient, high quality options for long-term skilling, benchmarked to internationally acceptable qualification standards, which will ultimately contribute to the creation of a highly skilled workforce.
6. Develop a network of quality instructors/trainers in the skill development ecosystem by establishing high quality teacher training institutions.
7. Leverage existing public infrastructure and industry facilities for scaling up skill training and capacity building efforts.
8. Offer a passage for overseas employment through specific programmes mapped to global job requirements and benchmarked to international standards.
9. Enable pathways for transitioning between the vocational training system and the formal education system, through a credit transfer system.
10. Promote convergence and co-ordination between skill development efforts of all Central Ministries/Departments/ States/implementing agencies.
11. Support weaker and disadvantaged sections of society through focused outreach programmes and targeted skill development activities.
12. Propogate aspirational value of skilling among youth, by creating social awareness on value of skill training.
13. Maintain a national database, known as the Labour Market Information System (LMIS), which will act as a portal for matching the demand and supply of skilled workforce in the country. The LMIS, will on the one hand provide citizens with vital information on skilling initiatives across the country. On the other, it will also serve as a platform for monitoring the performance of existing skill development programmes, running in every Indian state.

Institutional Mechanisms

There will be a National Skill Development Mission at the Centre to steer, drive and execute the Mission's objectives. Key institutional mechanisms for achieving the objectives of the Mission have been divided into three tiers. The Mission will consist of a Government Council at apex level, a Steering Committee and a Mission Directorate (along with an Executive Committee) as the executive arm of the Mission.

Mission Directorate will be supported by three other institutions: National Skill Development Agency (NSDA), National Skill Development Corporation (NSDC), and Directorate General of Training (DGT) – all of which will have linkages with Mission Directorate to facilitate smooth functioning of the national institutional mechanism. These three agencies would continue to lie under the umbrella of Ministry of Skill Development and Entrepreneurship.

At State level, States will be encouraged to create State Skill Development Missions (SSDM) along the lines of National Skill Development Mission with a Steering Committee and Mission Directorate at State level. States will in turn, be supported by District Committees at the functional tier.

Composition and functions of these bodies have been described as follows:

National Level

Mission Governing Council at Apex level will be headed by Prime Minister, Governing Council may also invite other CMs, other Union Ministers and relevant persons from academia and industry, depending on the agenda for discussion.

A Steering Committee, chaired by Minister incharge of Ministry of Skill Development and Entrepreneurship will be responsible for ensuring that implementation of Mission activities is done as per policies and decisions laid down by Governing Council. Secretary, Skill Development and Entrepreneurship will be Member Secretary of the Steering Committee. It will also consist of Secretaries of M/o Labour and Employment, M/o MSME, M/o Agriculture, M/o HRD, M/o Overseas Affairs, M/o HUPA and M/o Information Technology which are running large scale skill training programmes across the country.

Mission Directorate will have an ***Executive Committee***, chaired by Secretary, Skill ***Development and Entrepreneurship***, who will also act as Mission Director. Joint Secretaries of M/o Labour and Employment, M/o MSME, M/o of Finance, M/o of Rural Development, M/o Agriculture, M/o Human Resource Development, M/o Overseas Affairs, M/o HUPA and M/o Information Technology would be Members of the Executive Committee. Five Secretaries from the States handling skills department/ministry in the state on a rotational basis, will be members as well. Further, DG NSDA, MD NSDC, and DG (Training) would also be members. A Joint Secretary, nominated by Mission Director will act as Member Secretary of the Executive Committee. Joint Secretaries from relevant Central Ministries/ Departments which have initiated new skill development programmes will automatically become members of Executive Committee in order to ensure convergence of individual/sector specific goals with national and Mission objectives. Executive Committee will meet on a monthly basis. Mission Directorate, with Secretary, MSDE as Mission Director will support Executive Committee.

Functions of Executive committee are as follows:

- To resolve all inter-departmental execution issues.
- Set annual targets for all sub-missions, which will be created in areas requiring significant focus on an immediate basis in the skill landscape. Currently 7 sub-missions have been identified.
- Converge skilling activities across all sectors with national Mission objectives and skill gap findings.

Functions of Mission Directorate are as follows:

- To implement and monitor Mission activities at a national level. Mission Directorate will be supported by the administrative and financial wing of MSDE.
- To coordinate implementation of all decisions of Governing Council and Steering Committee.
- The power of allocation/re-allocation of resources to States/ implementing agencies, as well as approval of their Annual Action Plans, will fall within the purview of Mission Directorate.
- To ensure uniformity in quality, certification, norms of training, curriculum content, Aadhaar seeding, leveraging Jan Dhan accounts and social security schemes etc across all skill development programmes being implemented by all Ministries/ Departments.
- Coordinate and converge State efforts in order to align them with the broad national objectives outlined in the National Action Plan.
- Coordinate efforts and monitor performance of individual Sub-Missions, headed by their respective CEOs, to provide end-to-end solutions towards achieving the objectives of Sub-Missions.

- Create tie-ups with institutions worldwide to facilitate information sharing.
- Any other work assigned by Governing Council or Steering Committee.

NSDA will focus on two verticals of Quality Assurance and policy research in the skills space, It will operationalise a credible Quality Assurance Framework embedded in the National Skill Qualification Framework (NSQF) to align skilling outcomes to NSQF across the skills landscape. To improve synergy between Mission Directorate and NSDA, it is proposed that Secretary MSDE should also be designated as ex-officio Chairman of NSDA. This will enable Secretary to Chair National Skills Qualification Committee (NSQC) also in his capacity as Chairman NSDA and will help energies NSQC which is not only responsible for establishing a Quality Assurance framework embedded in NSQF in the skill space but also needs to provide a framework for certification, accreditation of training providers etc.

Other functions of NSDA will include:

- Operationalise and implement National Skill Qualification Framework (NSQF).
- To establish and operationalise a QA framework embedded in NSQF to improve consistency of outcomes in the skills landscape, which will include laying down a framework for training, assessment and certification processes and agencies in the country.
- To operationalise National Skills Qualification Committee (NSQC) to meet its objectives.
- Designing and implement the National Labour Market Information System.
- Develop national protocols for registration and accreditation of private training providers.
- Promote use of 'Skill India' logo on skill certificates by SSCs/ Agencies adhering to the QA framework.
- Anchor Prime Minister's Skill Development Fellow Programme.

National Skills Research Division (NSRD), under NSDA will be established to serve as the apex body for providing technical and research support to the Mission, This institution will act as a think-tank for Ministry of Skill Development and Entrepreneurship and be the core skill development hub, which will connect implementation of the Mission with academic research and data.

It will leverage expertise in Private domain and be headed by an economist/expert in the field of planning, with adequate domestic or international experience in skill development. The selection of the head of this division will be done through an empowered Search Committee consisting of:

Four key functions of the Division

- Research
- Policy Advisory/Inputs
- Careers Support
- Knowledge Exchange Networks

Other functions of NSDC

- Catalyse the creation of market-based, scalable business by providing funding through a combination of debt, equity and grants.
- Implementing skills voucher programe
- Driving engagement with industry and businesses.
- Promote centres of excellence for traingin of trainers in coordination with States and SSCs
- Initiating and incubating Sector Skills Councils (SSCs)

Directorate General of Training: The two verticals of Training and Apprenticeship under DGET, MoLE have been shifted to Ministry of Skill Development and Entrepreneurship from 16th April 2015. These two verticals will function through Directorate of Training and Directorate of Apprenticeship Training respectively under the Directorate General of Training under the Ministry of Skill Development and Entrepreneurship. It will be responsible for maintaining existing skill training structures in the country through National Council for Vocational Training (NCVT). Its large institutional framework consisting of ITIs, ATIs RVTIs and other national institutes will act as tools of execution for Mission activities.

State Level

States will be encouraged to create State Skill Development Missions (SSOM) along the same lines as National Skill Development Mission structure. Many States have already established SSDMs and others have started moving in this direction.

The organization structure of the State Skill Development Mission is to be decided by the respective States. It is however desirable that the highest body looking after the Development Mission is sufficiently empowered. National Mission will work towards empowering State Missions through financial and technical support.

Mission Strategy

National Skill Development Mission will initially consist of seven sub-missions under its purview, which could be added to/amended as per decision of Governing Council. The power to identify sub-missions in crucial areas which require immediate attention will lie with Governing Council chaired by Hon'ble Prime Minister. Executive guidelines and detailing of each sub-mission will be done by Executive Committee. Key focus areas of the sub-mission include: addressing the long-term and short-term skilling needs through revamp of existing institutional training framework and establishing new institutions, undertake sector specific skill training initiatives, ensure convergence of existing skill development programmes; leverage existing public infrastructure for skilling; focus on training of trainers, facilitate overseas employment, and promote sustainable livelihoods.

Sub-Missions have currently been proposed in priority areas. The number of sub-missions can be modified as per changing skill requirements and challenges. Each sub-mission will be headed by a Joint Secretary or Director level officer designated as CEO, sourced from the public or private sector who has a solid track record of implementing projects and achieving targets in a timely manner. The Sub-Mission's support team will consist of high performing individuals drawn from the public and private domains.

Financing

The implementation of skilling activities under the Mission will be as per the budget provisions of various schemes under their respective heads of account. The administrative expenses of the Mission will be borne from the budget of Ministry of Skill Development and Entrepreneurship. The IFD of the Ministry will function as the finance wing of the Mission. The Administrative support to the Mission will be provided by the Ministry.

Organisational Structure

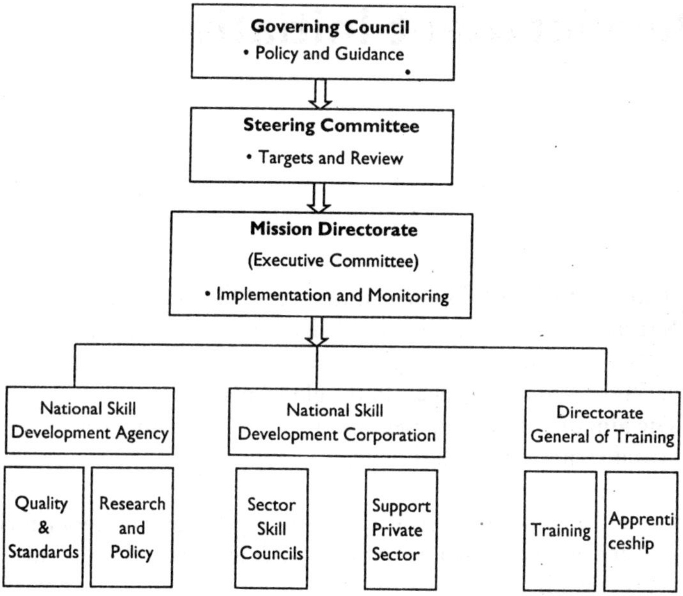

8

Vision for National Skill Development Initiative

National Skill Development Initiative will empower all individuals through improved skills, knowledge, nationally and internationally recognized qualifications to gain access to decent employment and ensure India's competitiveness in the global market.

The aim of skill development in the country is to support achieving rapid and inclusive growth through:

- Enhancing individuals' employability (wage/self employment) and ability to adapt to changing technologies and labour market demands.
- Improving productivity and living standards of the people.
- Strengthening competitiveness of the country.
- Attracting investment in skill development.

The objectives of the national policy on skill development are to:

- Create opportunities for all to acquire skills throughout life, and especially for youth, women and disadvantaged groups.
- Promote commitment by all stakeholders to own skill development initiatives.
- Develop a high-quality skilled workforce/entrepreneur relevant to current and emerging employment market needs
- Enable the establishment of flexible delivery mechanisms that respond to the characteristics of a wide range of needs of stakeholders.

- ***Scale of ambition:*** At present the capacity of skill development in India is around 3.1 million persons per year. The 11th Five Year Plan envisions an increase in that capacity to 15 million annually. India has target of creating 500 million skilled workers by 2022. Thus, there is a need for increasing capacity and capability of skill development programs.
- ***High inclusivity:*** The skill development initiatives will harness inclusivity and reduce divisions such as male/female, rural/urban, organized/unorganized employment and traditional/contemporary workplace.
- ***Dynamic and demand-based system planning:*** The skill development initiatives support the supply of trained workers who are adjustable dynamically to the changing demands of employment and technologies. This policy will promote excellence and will meet the requirements of knowledge economy.
- ***Choice, competition and accountability:*** The skill development initiative does not discriminate between private or public delivery and places importance on outcomes, users' choice and competition among training providers and their accountability.
- ***Policy coordination and coherence:*** The skill development initiatives support employment generation, economic growth and social development processes. Skill development policy will be an integral part of comprehensive economic, labour and social policies and programmes. A framework for better coordination among various Ministries, States, industry and other stakeholders will be established.

The following **operational strategies** will be adopted:

- ***Folding the future in:*** If we start from our current position, we are likely to extrapolate. Folding the future in allows us to innovate. Innovation is, therefore, an important element of the strategy.
- ***Skills framework must move to a system of equivalence to diploma and degree:*** National Vocational Qualification Framework (NVQF) will be created with an open/flexible system which will permit individuals to accumulate their knowledge and skills, and convert them through testing and certification into higher diplomas and degrees. NVQF will provide quality

assured various learning pathways having standards, comparable with any international qualification framework. NVQF will support lifelong learning, continuous upgradation of skills and knowledge.

- ***Skills must be bankable*:** The process of skill acquisition especially for the poor and needy persons will be made bankable. The effort would be to complement public investment with institutional/bank finance.
- ***Co-created solution and forging partnerships*:** We have to accepts a very asymmetric India as a starting point. Partnerships will be consciously promoted between Government, industry, local government, civil society institutions and all potential skill providers. Institutional mechanism and standing platforms will be created to ensure sustainability.
- ***Game-changing delivery/innovation*:** Availability of public institutions above the high school level, after class hours for skill development by the Private Sector, without disturbing the normal working, will be explored. Necessary regulations would be brought in by the local management authority of the particular education institution.

Core Operating Principles

- ***Government financial support must complement private investment*:** the Central Ministries must focus on areas where private investment in skilled development is unlikely to be available or forthcoming. The Government would aim at useful public-private partnerships.
- ***States as key actors*:** The State being the key actors in Skill Development would set up overarching integrated framework for action for Skill Development through State level Skill Development Mission.
- ***Deployment of funds*:** The fund would be deployed more for activities than for buildings and other hard assets. However, upgradation of machinery and equipment, teaching and learning aids will be a continuous process. Creation of infrastructure in latest technology, need-based new initiatives, creation of infrastructure in rural, remote and difficult areas will continue.
- ***Focus of modular courses, open architecture and short term courses:*** With fast changing skills in the labour market, focus

would be on short, relevant and effective courses that would get candidates into the workplace. They will be welded through NVQF to maintain dynamism and open to feedback.

- ***Separate financing from delivery*:** Today Government funds are only available for government delivery. National Skill Development Corporation will support Private skill development initiatives. Following financing options will be explored:

  a) *Link financing to outcomes*: Today public and private training is financed largely on inputs viz. number of courses, number of students, faculty, etc. efforts would be made to move towards Government financing linked to placement ratios and outcomes.

  b) *Focus funding on candidates*: the focus would be on funding the candidates rather than institutions to create choice. This could be structured as a scholarship, skill voucher, outcome based reimbursement, etc.

- ***Create infrastructure for on-the-job-training and encourage apprenticeships*:** The enabling infrastructure for large number of formal apprentices needs to be built that includes modification to the Apprentices Act, 1961.
- ***Publicise rating and outcome information on training institutions*:** A framework of accreditation and infrastructure for information dissemination around measurable criteria on institutions will be created. Rating of public and private institutions would be put on public domain.
- ***Effective assessment and credible certification:*** Quality assured learning credible assessment and certification will be developed. This will allow employers to use the certificate as a proxy to fast track job applicants.
- ***Restructure employment exchanges as career guidance centres:*** Employment Exchanges will be restructured as career guidance centres to channelize candidates into jobs, apprenticeships and training.
- ***Expand formal employment:*** Formal employment is not only fiscally attractive but more amenable to financing innovations. This will require a review of existing State and Central legislations which encourage informal and unorganized employment.

Approach to Deliverables

- ***Diversity of skills:*** There is a need to identify, catalog and project the range and depthof skills e.g. traditional, industrial-era and post-industrial era skills to understand and present the vast array of skills that individuals can choose from.
- ***Talent pool:*** The ultimate measure is the "500 million" skilled people. Skill inventory along with its various level and grades will be created.
- ***Employment outcomes:*** Skill training must ensure a job for those who seek it. The placement ratio will be monitored and placed in the public domain by agencies involved in skill training.

9

National Policy for Skill Development 2015

Vision

To create an ecosystem of empowerment by Skilling on a large Scale at Speed with high Standards and to promote a culture of innovation based entrepreneurship which can generate wealth and employment so as to ensure sustainable livelihood for all citizens in the country.

Mission

The mission is to

- Create a demand for skilling across the country;
- Correct and align skilling with required competencies;
- Connect the supply of skilled human resources with sectoral demands;
- Certify and assess in alignment with global and national standards; and
- Catalyse an ecosystem wherein productive and innovative entrepreneurship germinates, sustains and grows leading to creation of a more dynamic entrepreneurial economy and more formal wage employment.

Objectives

The core objective of the Policy is to empower the individual, by enabling her/him to realize their full potential through a process of lifelong learning where comprtencies are accumulated via instruments such as credible certifications, credit accumulation and transfer, etc. As individuals grow, the society and nation also benefit from their productivity and growth. This will involve:

i. Make quality vocational training aspirational for both youth and employers whereby youth sees it as a matter of choice and employer acknowledges the productivity linked to skilled workforce by paying the requisite premium.
ii. Ensure both vertical and horizontal pathways to skilled workforce for futher growth by providing sceamless integration of skill training with formal education
iii. Focus on an outcome based approach towards quality skilling that on one hand results in increased employability and better livelihoods for individuals, and on the other hand translates into improved productivity across primary, secondary and tertiary sectors.
iv. Increase the capacity and quality of training infrastructure and trainers to ensure equitable and easy access to every citizens.
v. Address human resource needs by aligning supply of skilled workers with sectoral requirements of industry and the country's strategic priorities including flagship programmes like Make in India.
vi. Establish an IT based information system for aggregating demand and supply of skilled workforce which can help in matching and connecting supply with demand.
vii. Promote national standards in the skilling space through active involvement of employers in setting occupational standards, helping develop curriculum, providing apprenticeship opportunities, participating in assessments, and providing gainful employment to skilled workforce with adequate compensation.
viii. Operationalise a well defined quality assurance framework aligned with global standards to facilitate mobility of labour.
ix. Leverage modern technology to ensure scale, access and outreach, in addition to ease of delivering content and monitoring results.
x. Recognize the value of on the job training, by making apprenticeships in actual work environments an integral part of all skill development efforts.
xi. Ensure that the skilling needs of the socially and geographically disadvantaged and marginalized groups (like the SCs, STs, OBCs, minorities, differently abled persons etc) are appropriately taken care of.

xii. Promote increased participation of women in the workforce through appropriate skilling and gender mainstreaming of training.

xiii. Promote commitment and ownership of all stakeholders towards skill development and create an effective coordination mechanism.

Policy Framework for Skill Development

The policy frame work has been developed to accomplish the vision of Skill India by adhering to the objectives mentioned. The framework outlines eleven major paradigms and enablers to achieve these objectives of skilling India:

- Aspiration and Advocacy
- Capacity
- Quality
- Synergy
- Mobilization and Engagement
- Global Partnerships
- Outreach
- ICT Enablement
- Trainers and Assessors
- Inclusivity
- Promotion of skilling among women

Aspiration and Advocacy

The need of the hour is to make skill development aspirational for boys and girls in our country. For skill training to be looked at as a matter of choice, it must

- Provide vertical growth pathways on the lines of the general education system, so that skill education and training is also seen as a valid route to earn degree and diplomas, and consequently to position of authority linked to such qualifications; and
- be associated with growth and sustainable livelihood pathways; and
- have a causal relationship with increased income for skilled workforce.

A National Campaign will be launched within three months to create awareness and a positive pro skilling environment. Communication packages and kits will be standardized to ensure quality, and made available in all local languages with focused promotion through skill ambassadors including eminent personalities. State wise camps will be organized for skills awareness and mobilization. Social media will be effectively used to amplify the campaign and build publicity. A TV channel and a national community radio frequency dedicated to skill will be promoted to enable communication and dissemination of information and opportunities relating to skills on a regular basis. The Skill India logo will also be used to promote the value of a skilled workforce and create momentum for skilling amongst the youth.

National Skills Universities and institutes will be promoted in partnership with States as centres of excellence for skill development and training of trainers, either as de novo institutions or as a part of existing university landscape. It is desired that these institutions become as aspirational for candidates as other premier institutes around the country. These institutions, apart from skilling candidates through affiliates and training the trainers, will also conduct extensive research to enhance the quality and delivery of skill training by keeping abreast with least developments in the skills space.

Skilling will be integrated with formal education by introducing vocational training classes linked to the local economy from class nine onwards in at least 25 per cent of the schools, over the next five years. Seamless integration of vocational training in formal education is expected to ignite student interest. All NSQF compliant assessment and certification bodies will be competent to provide support to the School Boards for assessment and certification of the skilling component of vocational education and training, wherever required.

Skilling will be increasingly integrated with higher education with polytechnics offering NSQF aligned vocational courses and Bachelor of Vocational Studies degrees. These courses will be aligned to a credit framework which can provide horizontal and vertical mobility. Further, at least 25 per cent of all existing institutions of higher education would offer add on career oriented courses with specialized skills at an appropriate NSQF level within the next five years.

The ITI qualifications will be linked to formal educational qualification at appropriate level through suitable languages/bridge courses as necessary in consultation with State/Central boards of education. The existing ITS and polytechnics will be modernized with courses and curriculum that are eligible to the emerging competency based demand in the market. Technology would be leveraged for designing curricula and developing pedagogical techniques. ITIs interface with industry will be promoted to enhance apprenticeship opportunities, improve relevance of training and increase employability of trainees. Industry is expected to take a lead role in running ITIs through Institute Management Committees (IMCs) which will be given autonomy to implements decisions in the interest of better training outcomes. Performance rating of ITIs will also be promoted based on outcome linked parameters and trainee/employer feedback

Government will promote use of certified, skilled manpower for its work and projects through enabling provisions in their contracts. Industry will also be encouraged to follow suit and pay skill premium to skilled and semi skilled workers. The companies will also be asked to indicate the percentage of certified, skilled workforce in their units as a part of their annual report.

To further the aspiration and respect associated with skilling, National Skill Awards will be instituted in clone association with major stakeholders. Participation of India at international platforms will be encouraged to showcase the skilling talent in the country. Moreover, a 'National Skills Day' will be declared to annually commemorate and celebrate skilling through skill fairs and camps across the country.

Counselling and guidance have emerged as the biggest challenges in the skill space today. Good counseling will be useful to create aspiration, reduce the attrition rates during training and employment by helping candidates make informed choices. The vast network of existing Post Offices and Citizen Service Centers (CSCs) would be leveraged with industry support to create such a support system for the youth. Further, the network of 2.85 lakh Youth Clubs/Mahila Mandals of Nehru Yuva Kendras with presence in 623 districts would also facilitate in providing counselling and guidance to the youth of the country about various skilling programmes and opportunities. Similarly, the cross country network of volunteers of Nehru Yuva Kendra Sangathan and National Service Scheme will also be utilized to create awareness and build a favourable pro skilling environment among the youth in the country. These agencies will be provided with necessary brochures and other material for dissemination of requirement information through its volunteers among the target audience.

The Prime Minister's Skill Development Fellow Scheme will be introduced to tap talented, young individuals who will work with the State and District administration to spread awareness about skill development, identify the local needs and steer skill development efforts in the regional.

Capacity

The annual skilling in the country was estimated at around 7 million in 2014. In the current landscape, capacity is being created by private sector training organizations, industry in house training, government and private Industrial Training Institutes (ITIs), Advanced Training institutes (ATIs), tool rooms and in schools, colleges and polytechnics. For all existing and new capacity that will be generated, the focus will move from inputs to outcomes of skill training that include employability and placements of trainees. Incentives will be linked to placement in all training institutions. For Government supported schemes, funding will be linked to outcomes of the training programmes.

Government will support the creation and use of infrastructure in both public and private domain through appropriate equality, grant and loan support. It will continue to encourage entrepreneurs to enter into the skill training space by providing milestone linked funding support through existing and new institutional mechanisms.

Special focus will be laid on youth who do not wish to continue with school or higher education so that they are provided skills for other sustainable livelihood options. Special programmes will be initiated for providing skill training to those who have eight years or more of schooling. Separate skill courses, aligned to the appropriate NSQF levels, will be held in existing schools/centres, during evening hours to provide alternate career pathway to these students. NSQF as a means to integrate and provide multiple pathways between general and vocational education will help school drop outs make choices about vocational courses.

State Government would be encouraged to setup Kaushal Vardhan Kendras (KVKs) at panchayat level for mobilizing and imparting skills pertaining to local employment/livelihood opportunities to school drop outs, adolescent girls, housewives and rural youth. Each KVK will be linked to the nearest ITI/MSI/ATI for capacity building, curriculum development, assessment and certification.

Private Sector initiative in skilling will be encouraged and would be entrusted to NSDC to create skilling capacity in the country.

Quality

'One National One Standards' should become the mantra to ensure that national standards and quality for skilling are globally aligned and Indian youth can aspire to secure local, national and international job opportunities. Quality of training can be measured by competency outcomes and employability of trainees. The following parameters have been identified for improving quality:

- Quality assurance framework embedded in NSQF
- Market relevant training programmes
- Recognition of prior learning
- Curriculum alignment
- National Certification Framework
- Employability skills
- Placements

Quality Assurance

A Quality Assurance (QA) framework embedded in NSQF will be finalized within next one year. This will build trust and confidence in the system by putting in place mechanisms that ensure the qualifications (and related training) produce consistent quality outcomes, and are relevant to the labour market. It will ensure that training providers have the capacity to deliver training that meets quality requirements. The QA framework will improve the consistency of outcomes linked to certification and consequently improve the status of skills training. It would also lay down the framework for independent assessment and certification system in the country.

All formal and vocational education including skill training will have to align themselves with NSQF by December 2018. It is a nationally integrated education and competency based skill framework that will provide for multiple pathways, horizontal as well as vertical, within vocational education, vocational training, general education and technical education, thus linking one level of learning to another higher level. This would facilitate both horizontal and vertical mobility with formal education on outcome base equivalence linked to a uniform credit framework. A legal framework to support NSQF will also be put in place.

Recognition of Prior Learning (RPL)

RPL is the key instrument which can help map the existing skills in the unorganized sector and integrate the informal sector to the formal skilling landscape. The RPL framework is an outcome based qualification framework linked to NSQF against which prior learning through formal/informal channels would be assessed and certified. The RPL process would include pre assessment, skill gap training and final assessment leading to certification of existing skills in an individual. The RPL certification would be at par with the certifications following various skill trainings in the country. It will provide both horizontal and vertical pathways to individuals for acquiring additional skills for better livelihoods. Adequate resources will be earmarked under various government schemes for equitable access to RPL programmes. The government will provide detailed guidelines for RPL initiatives which will ensure quality and consistent outcomes.

Creating a dynamic and demand driven Curriculum Framework

The curricula development will be promoted through sector mentor committee which will include representatives from concerned SSCs sector experts and relevant academia, so as to ensure that the curricula is in sync with emerging market demands and aligned to latest NOSs and QPs. The curricula should also take into account the latest teaching aids which can be used to disseminate quality training on a large scale. The curricula will need to be reviewed every three years to align itself with the dynamic market needs. In addition, industry will be allowed to run high employment potential courses through appropriate affiliation framework.

National Certification Framework

Presently, the National Council for Vocational Training (NCVT) constituted in 1956, provides a national framework for setting curricula for various vocational courses, and also prescribe standards for equipment, scale of space, duration of courses, methods of training, conducting All India Trade Tests and awarding National Trade Certificates. NCVT will be further strengthened by scaling up industry representation through SSCs and laying down a national framework for all certification in the skill space through an autonomous body.

Employability Skills

Language, basis IT and financial literacy is an integral past of most job roles in the economy today. Further, life skills are also an integral to a successful livelihood. Accordingly, all skill training programmes shall include basic modules of computer literacy, finance, language and soft skills like etiquettes, apprenticlating gender diversity in workplace, building positive health attitudes, social and life skills to enable the youth to be employable and market ready.

Placements

The most critical outcome of skill training is employment, whether self or wage employment. To assess quality of skill training, this critical outcome will need to be monitored objectively. Employment tracking of individuals for at least one year, post skill training will be made mandatory under all skill programmes

Synergy

Skill development programmes being implemented by various ministries/ departments/agencies of the Central Government have different norms as regards the eligibility criteria, duration of training, maximum amount for training, outcomes, monitoring and tracking mechanism etc. This multiplicity of norms and parameters results in avoidable diffulties in implementation and makes it difficult to evaluate the performance of the skill development programmes across the Central Government in an objective manner.

Ministry of Skill Development and Entrepreneurship (MSDE), which has been set up to coordinate skill development efforts in the country will within three month, notify common norms for rationalization of Central Government Schemes on Skill Development. The norms shall include standards for inputs/output, funding/cost norms, third party certification and assessment cost etc across various skill development programmes while allowing flexibility to meet the requirements of different parts of the country/different socio economic groups. However, different ministries will be free to frame schemes at their discretion to meet local/sectoral needs while adhering to common norms.

Mobilization and Engagement

Industry needs to be closely involved in providing job opportunities to the skilled workforce. Industry will be encouraged to increasingly move towards employing only certified skilled people. In addition, employers need to realize the compensation paid across different levels of skills to award a skill premium for increased productivity as a result of higher skills.

Skill development is shared responsibility of both Government as well as industry. Since industry is one of the major stakeholders, it needs to actively contribute to the cause of skill development. The industry should earmark at least 2 per cent of its payroll bill (including for contract labour) for skill development activities in their respective sector. These funds can be channelized for skill development activities either through the respective SSCs or through National Skill Development Fund (NSDF).

Global Partnerships

The main objective of global partnerships and international collaboration is to leverage best practices from across the world. Such collaborations will immensely enrich domestic training programmes by enhancing their quality through learning from successful international models of vocationalization of education, engaging with industry, etc. Institutional arrangements through joint working groups, secretariats, etc will be established for regular exchange of knowledge, experiences, research findings, teaching and learning materials, and innovations in skill development.

Foreign Governments, corporate and agencies will also be encouraged to set up skill centres and universities as well as participate in content creation, design of curricula and delivery of training. Exchange and capacity building programmes for teachers, administrators and students will be facilitated.

Government would promote a skills training ecosystem that would also enable training and placement of Indian boys and girls in overseas jobs. The ageing developed world is expected to face a huge skill shortage while our country has the potential to reap its demographic advantage and export skilling labour to the world. A focused team would be formulated for identification of countries and trades where skill shortages exit or, are likely to develop in near future.

Currently there are about 14 million Indians overseas, 70 per cent of whom are unskilled or semiskilled labourers. Due to several reasons such as lack of skills, inadequate information, lack of knowledge of basis language, etc, they often have to work in adverse circumstances with biased terms of employment. To address the existing issues faced by Indian labourers abroad the government will further enhance the scheme of skill up gradation and pre departure orientation training to emigrant workers.

ICT Enablement

Promotion of only brick and mortar facilities will not ensure the speed and scale desired to transform the skill development efforts The use of technology will be leveraged to scale up training facilities, enable access to remote areas and increase cost effectiveness of delivery of vocational training. Government will also look to support innovative products, solutions and models that address critical gaps in skill ecosystem in an effective manner. Use of existing available networks such as the widespread Optical Fiber Network will be optimized.

Inclusivity it is necessary to promote skill development initiatives that will ensure inclusivity, irrespective of gender, location, caste, sector etc. one of the key objectives is to safeguard the skilling needs of SCs, STs, OBCs, minorities, and differently abled persons, as well as those living in difficult geographical pockets.

Government attaches high priority to socio economic growth of rural areas since India lives in her villages. Adequate focus will be given to youth from deprived households by establishing skill development centres in areas which are underserved.

The border, hilly and difficult areas, including North Eastern states, J&K, and the hilly forested areas of central and eastern India, face additional challenges arising from inadequate infrastructure, poor investment and low industrial opportunities. Special attention needs to be given to youth residing in these regions to address their needs for employment and employability. In order to provide more equitable access across the country, special efforts including earmarking of funds for establishing training facilities in different regions and need based subsidization of skill training for disadvantaged groups will be initiated. Natural aptitude of youth will also be kept in view implementing training programmes in these geographies.

Governance Structure and Financing

Governance Structure

Ministry of Skill Development and Entrepreneurship has been created to fulfill the vision of a 'Skilled India' where human resource development is the primary focus. MSDE will be responsible for coordination with all concerned for evolving an appropriate skill development framework, removal of disconnect between demand for, and supply of, skilled manpower, skill up gradation, building of new skills, innovative thinking and talents for existing and future jobs.

MSDE will also play the lead role in ensuring the implementation of the National Policy for Skill Development 2015.

The objectives and targets under the National policy will be met in mission mode approach. The **National Skill Development Mission** will be launched to implement and coordinate all skilling efforts in the country towards the objectives laid down in the policy. The Mission will be housed in MSDE and the key institutional mechanism for achieving the objectives of the Mission will be divided into three tier structure at the Centre to steer, drive and execute the Mission's objectives. The Mission will Directorate (along with an Executive Committee) as the executive arm of the Mission. At State levels, States will be encouraged to creat State Skill Development Missions (SSDM) along the lines of National Skill Development Mission with a Steering Committee and Mission Directorate at State level. State will in turn, be supported by District Committees at the functional tier.

Mission Directorate will be supported by three other institutions: National Skill Development Agency (NSDA). National Skill Development Corporation (NSDC), and Directorate General of Training (DGT) – all of which have horizontal/vertical linkages with Mission Directorate to facilitate smooth functioning of the national institutional mechanism.

National Skill Development Agency (NSDA); NSDA was set up as a Society in June 2013. NSDA will focus on the two verticals of Quality Assurance and policy research in the skills space. It will be majorly responsible for the following activities:

- Operationalise and implement National Skill Qualification Framework (NSQF).
- Establish and Operationalise a QA framework embedded in NSQF to improve consistency of outcomes in the skill landscape, which include laying down a framework for training assessment and certification process and agencies in the country.
- Operationalise National Skill Qualification Committee (NSQC) to meet its objectives.
- Design and implement the National Labour Market Information System.
- Develop national protocols for registration and accreditation of private training providers.
- Promote use of 'Skill India' logo on skill certificates by SSCs/ Agencies adhering to the QA framework.
- Anchor Prime Minister's Skill Development Fellow Programme.

National Skill Research Division (NSRD), under NSDA will be established to serve as the apex division for providing technical and research support to the Mission. This division will act as a think tank for MSDE and be the core skill development hub, which will connect implementation of the Mission with academic research and data. Its four key functions will include research, policy advisory/inputs, career support and knowledge exchange networks.

National Skill Development Corporation (NSDC): NSDC, a Public Private Partnership was set up in 2008 as a Section 25 under Companies Act, 1956 with shareholding of GOI 49 per cent and private sector 51 per cent. It will be the nodal organization for all private sector initiatives in the short term skilling space. Its mandate will primarily include

- Catalyse the creation of market based, scalable business by providing funding through a combination of debt, equity and grants
- Implementing skills voucher programme
- Driving engagement with industry and businesses
- Promote centres of excellence for training of trainers in coordination with States and SSCs
- Initiating and incubating Sector Skills Councils (SSCs)
- Discharge any other function as may be assigned to it by the Ministry.

Directorate General of Training: The two verticals of Training and Apprenticeship Training under DGET, MoLE have been shifted to MSDE from 16th April 2015. Its large institutional framework consisting of ITIs, ATIs and other national institutes will act as tools of execution for Mission activities. Other functions will include:

- Setting up framework for structure of courses, assessment, curricula creation, affiliation and accreditation of institutes, under NCVT
- Develop national standards on syllabi, equipment, scale of space, duration of courses and methods of training
- Advise on training policy in its network of training institutes
- Coordinate functioning of Industrial Training Institutes (ITIs)
- Run training programmes for training of trainers/instructors
- Run special institutes for training of women
- Leverage field infrastructure for strong industry interface in all facts of training, including on the job training

- Provide technical support to vocational education across the country
- Anchor and operationalise Apprentices Act, 1961 as overhauled by comprehensive amendments in Dec, 2014
- Operationalise various training schemes through ITIs and Vocational Training Providers (VTPs)

Sector Skill Councils (SSCs): In order to ensure that skill development efforts being made by all stakeholders in the system are in accordance with actual needs of industry, SSCs are being set up. SSCs are industry led and industry governed bodies, which will help link the requirements of industry with appropriately trained manpower.

Sector Skill Councils will discharge the following functions:

- Identification of skill development needs including preparing a catalogue of type of skills, range and depth of skills to facilitate individuals to chose from them.
- Development of a sector skill development plan and maintain skill inventory.
- Determining skills/competency standards and qualifications and getting them notified as per NSQF.
- Standardization of affiliation, accreditation, examination and certification process in accordance with NSQF as determined by NSQC. May also conduct skill based assessment and certification for QP/NOS aligned training programmes.
- Participation in the setting up of affiliation, accreditation, examination and certification norms for their respective sectors.
- Plan and facilitate the execution of Training of Trainers along with NSDC and States.
- Promotion of academies of excellence.
- Will lay special emphasis on the skilling needs of ST/SC, differently abled and minority populations.
- SSCs shall ensure that the person trained and skilled in accordance with the norms laid down by them are assured of employment at decent wages.

Financing

Public funds (comprised of funding by Central government, state government and grant based schemes) are finite and will not be abled to cover the magnitude of the challenge of Skilling India, hence alternative sources of funds are required. Therefore, all stakeholders, the Government both at Centre and States, the enterprise – public and private, and the direct beneficiary – the individual, would contribute in mobilizing financial or in kind resources for skill development. The success of the policy will depend upon the quantum of resources mobilized from all stakeholders.

National Skill Development Fund (NSDF) has been set up by Government of India with the objective of encouraging skill development in the country. A public Trust set up by Government of India is the custodian of the Fund. The Fund acts as a receptacle for all donations, contribution in cash or kind from all contributors (including Government, multilateral organizations, corporations etc) for furtherance of the objectives of the Fund.

All government schemes across sectors will be encouraged to apportion a certain percentage (10 per cent) of the scheme budget towards skilling of human resources in local regions in the required sector. These funds cold be used for implementation directly or be routed through NSDF. Government may consider other options including cess etc. to raise funds for meeting the requirements of this sector.

A Credit Guarantee Fund for skill development and a 'National Credit Guarantee Trustee Company' (NCGTC) has been set up to support the initative of loans for the purpose of skilling and will be used to leverage credit financing in the skill landscape. It will be further expanded to ensure greater outreach and access to all citizens.

Monitoring and Evaluation

The National Policy for Skill Development has been structured as an outcome oriented policy. It is therefore desirable that there should be regular monitoring and evaluation of the initiatives to ensure that best practice can be scaled and corrective measured can be introduced. The main idea of having a robust monitoring and evaluation mechanism is to ensure successful implementation of the policy initiatives.

Government desires to set up a 'Policy Implementation Unit' (PIU) so as to review the implementation of progress of the various initiatives under this policy. The PIU will be housed in MSDE with Secretary as the Chairperson and representation from NITI Aayog.

The PIU will be made responsible to the NSDM. It will present its reports, findings and the way forward to the steering Committee of the

Mission every quarter. The PIU will be the main body overlooking the Steering Committee of the Mission every quarter. The PIU will be the main body overlooking the implementation of policy.

Impact Assessment: For the purpose of undertaking impact assessment, annual as well as five year targets will be set for each stakeholder by the PIU. Impact assessment will be undertaken to ensure that the targets are met well within the time frame. The stakeholders will also be subject to a quarterly review. For the purpose of impact assessment, the following monitoring indicators, amongst others, are prescribed:

- Number/registrations of youth interested in skilling
- Number of youth registered in training programmes
- Number of youth assessed and certified by regulator authorities
- Placement rate of skilled trainees
- Number of accredited/affiliated training provides/centres
- Number of certified trainers, sector wise
- Number of certified assessories, sector wise
- Number of job role for which QPs and NOS have been developed
- Existing public infrastructure leveraged for training
- Number of skilled persons engaged in overseas employment
- Reduction in sectoral demand and supply gap
- Amount of private funds mobilized for encouraging groups enrolled in training programmes
- Percentage of skilled youth that are self employed
- Infrastructure dedicated for entrepreneurship courses
- Percentage of socially and geographically disadvantaged group engaged in self employment

With the help of the PIU, it will be easier to monitor the implementation of the policy initiatives and take corrective measures in case of non compliance. A mid term review of the policy will be undertaken based on impact assessment by a third party. The policy can be considered for review after five years, based on learning from implementation of the policy.

Break Up of Incremental Requirement Across Sectors

S. No.	Sector	Employment base in 2013 (million)	Project Employment by 2022 (million)	Incremental Human Resource Requirement (2013–22)
1	Auto and Auto Components	10.98	14.88	3.9
2	Beauty and Wellness	4.21	14.27	10.06
3	Food Processing	6.98	11.38	4.4
4	Media and Entertainment	0.4	1.3	0.9
5	Handlooms and Handicrafts	11.65	17.79	6.14
6	Leather and Leather Goods	3.09	6.81	3.72
7	Domestic Help	6	10.88	4.88
8	Gems and Jewellery	4.6	8.23	3.59
9	Telecommunication	2.08	4.16	2.08
10	Tourism, Hospitality & Travel	6.96	13.44	6.48
11	Furniture and Furnishing	4.11	11.29	7.18
12	Building, Construction and Real Estate	45.42	76.55	31.13
13	IT and ITES	2.96	5.12	2.16
14	Construction Material and Building Hardware	8.3	11	2.7
15	Textile and Clothing	15.23	21.54	6.31
16	Healthcare	3.59	7.39	3.8

(Continued)

(Continued)

17	Security	7	11.83	4.83
18	Agriculture	240.4	215.6	24.8
19	Education/skill development	13.02	17.31	4.29
20	Transportation and Logistics	16.74	28.4	11.66
21	Electronics and IT Hardware	4.33	8.94	4.61
22	Pharma and Life Sciences	1.86	3.58	1.72
23	BFSI	2.55	4.25	1.7
24	Retail	38.6	55.95	17.35
	Grand Total	461.1	581.89	120.79

Incremental Human Resource Requirements Across States (2013-22)

State	*Incremental HR Requirement Total 2012–22*
Andhra Pradesh	10871315
Arunachal Pradesh	147046
Assam	1234357
Chhattisgarh	3043736
Delhi	6341921
Goa	227261
Gujarat	5756711
Haryana	93268
Himachal	1206379
Jammu and Kashmir	1122787
Jharkhand	4452801
Karnataka	8476134
Kerala	2956896
Madhya Pradesh	7816045
Maharashtra	15522185
Manipur	233446
Meghalaya	248954
Mizoram	140188
Nagaland	97382
Odisha	3345584
Punjab	2899005
Rajasthan	4242438
Sikkim	147821
Tamil Nadu	13552000
Tripura	259330
Uttar Pradesh	11011055
Uttarakhand	2061143
West Bengal	9342561
Grand Total	120334478

10

Skill India to Go Far

In the words of Pushpa Despande, an analyst with AICC India, has an enormous demographic dividend. By 2026, nearly 65 per cent of our population will be between 15-64 years (with 35 per cent being below 35). Given that, the country is poised to become the world's single destination for skilled human resources. However, only 25 per cent of India's graduates, less than 10 per cent of MBA graduates and 17 per cent of engineers are employable (i.e., they have the necessary skill set to be employed by industries across sectors). Also, a vast majority of our population works in the informal sector, with little quantifiable skills. Consequently, our much hailed demographic dividend also happens to be a "demographic time bomb". India needs to aggressively invest in providing skills to its youth to capitalise on this untapped potential.

The Ministry of Skill Development and Entrepreneurship (MSDE), which was established to upgrade the UPA government's skill development infrastructure, the National Skill Development Agency (NSDA) and the National Skill Development Corporation (NSDC), a step in the right direction. This was especially so because despite their best intentions, the UPA governments had ended up reducing the grand aim of skill development to select training programs undertaken by various ministries and departments. Half-hearted attempts were made to streamline these programs, but there was no clear focus on skill development. The MSDE promised to bring cohesiveness and unity of purpose to skill development in India. However, apart from Prime Minister Narendra Modi's much publicity on skill development, the NDA government has done much.

Given that it was to be a nodal point for the coordination of all skill efforts across India, much was expected of the MSDE's "Common

Norms" (subsequently amended in May 2016), which were to bring about uniformity and standardisation in the implementation of various skill development schemes by different central ministries and departments. The ministry's own flagship program, the Pradhan Mantri Kaushal Vikas Yojana (PMKVY) still does not adhere to the common norms. The PMKVY does not have standardized minimum hours, training cost norms, funding norms or input standard norms.

Furthermore, the two bodies responsible for certifying people, the National Council of Vocational Training and the Assessment Agencies empanelled by the Sector Skills Councils, work at odds with one other. They follow dichotomous norms, be it with regard to hours of training, competency standards, assessment norms or certification. This defeats the idea of a unified nationwide skill certification, without which employers won't have a common metric of gauging the skill set of potential employees.

The PMKVY was designed so that the government would fund agencies to train people (Rs 10,000 was given for each individual trained). However, the government has not set up any monitoring or evaluation mechanisms to gauge the efficacy or the quality of training, thus reducing the scheme to mere statistical data. Consequently, a whooping Rs 1,500 crore was spent hastily and without clarity on outcomes.

Realising the enormity of the issue the NDA switched to funding 600 Kaushal Kendras and guaranteed them steady business. Firstly, the NDA has made the eligibility criterion so rigid that only a few companies are qualified, which opens the door for corruption and an exclusivist ecosystem. Secondly, by taking upon itself the responsibility of providing students, the NDA has removed any incentive for these Kendras to be genuinely interested in being quality institutions of skill development, since they need not be competitive to be attractive options for students.

The vision of skilling India has been further blurred by the way the NDA is managing it. Originally, the NSDA was designed to be an independent regulatory authority for quality assurance of skill development. The NDA has relegated the NSDA under MSDE and instead of an independent director general at the NSDA, it is led by a joint secretary within the ministry (thereby eliminating any scope for an honest appraisal of skilling programmes). Furthermore, both the NSDA and the NSDC have the same chairperson, which is clearly a conflict of interest, for one body is meant to implement the schemes for skilling and the other to regulate them. Adding to this, the PMKVY, which is also managed by the NSDC, is managed by another joint secretary.

Everyone in this swamp of institutions functions in independent silos, which has obviously resulted in severe conflicts of ideas and functions. How can we expect the MSDE to coordinate the skill agenda for the country when it cannot even coordinate or streamline itself?

It's highly unlikely that India will capitalise on its demographic dividend if the current state of affairs continues. There are no innovative and radical strategies being deployed to skill India, nor is there any evidence of a framework to operationalise this.

11

Skill Assessment: Policy, Practice and Capacity

Skills assessment in India is a rapidly evolving sector. Assessment can verify that individuals have the skills needed to perform a particular job and that the learning programme undertaken has delivered education at a given standard. It enables individuals to be benchmarked against their peers. It also has more intrinsic value in creating opportunities to motivate students and to give feedback. Assessment is closely linked to certification, as individuals often have the opportunity to gain a recognised certificate if they pass an assessment; certificates can provide a platform from which to progress to other areas of learning, to get a job or to progress within their existing careers.

With the current emphasis on skills development in India, increased focus on methods of assessment is inevitable. The scale and diversity of the Indian education system provides significant challenges in terms of training assessors and ensuring both the quality and the comparability of assessments.

The ILO and British council researchers in this paper offer a starting point from which to analyse the skills assessment sector, with a particular focus on three states: Haryana, Maharashtra and Odisha. The paper also focuses primarily on aspects of third party assessment, including funding; assessor recruitment and resourcing; skills gaps in the assessor workforce; assessment processes; quality assurance; and certification and placement. Finally, the paper makes recommendations for further development of the Indian skills assessment sector.

The information in this paper is derived from a combination of desk research and stakeholder consultation. Desk research included a review of international engagement with India's skills sector (including by the UK), evaluation of programme and initiative objectives as well as evidence of success and lessons learned and a review of policy and regulation within the Indian skills landscape, with special reference to the three states noted above.

Skills Development, Policy and Governance

The complexity and duplication of the regulatory and governance framework surrounding vocational and technical education in India means that initiatives and programmes are still occurring in silos, and the development of third party assessment has been no different. There are a number of assessment agencies which sit under the two key schemes; the Modular Employability Scheme - Skill Development Initiative (MES-SDI) and the Standard Training Assessment and Rewards (STAR). Further ministries are also implementing training programmes that are now introducing the requirement for third party assessment requirements, such as the Aajeevika Skill Development Programme (ASDP) and the Employment Skills Training & Placement Program (ESTP) under the National Urban Livelihoods Mission, which draw on certification from either the National Council for Vocational Training (NCVT) or Sector Skills Councils (SSC). Each programme is run differently and has distinct processes, which is limiting the potential coherence of assessor standards and performance. For agencies, it is also challenging in terms of reporting and administration.

The creation of the National Skills Qualifications Committee (NSQC) and implementation of the National Skill Qualification Framework (NSQF) is likely to have a significant impact on the role, remit and endorsement of SSCs. Additional pressure is being placed on existing systems of skill assessment and quality assurance by the NSQF, which is also raising issues around the respective roles of and relationships between the National Skill Development Agency (NSDA), National Skill Development Corporation (NSDC) and Sector Skill Councils (SSCs). The outcome of the recent elections has also seen the creation of the new Ministry of Skill Development and Entrepreneurship, which is likely to result in further changes to institutional arrangements in the sector.

The shifting targets and policy objectives are also having an impact on the quality of assessments: quality requirements for assessment agencies under the MES-SDI scheme have relaxed over time; this is thought by agencies to be due to the volume of agencies required and the haste with which policy decisions have been made.

The shift in focus from placement to certification and placement that has occurred in the Aajeevika scheme indicates the emphasis on onward progression of candidates, past the initial employment placement. By providing certification and placement, the scheme can satisfy both employers (who can have the assurances of certification) and candidates (who receive a job). This shift has also occurred in the recent MES-SDI scheme update, which now places financial incentives on training providers achieving placement for trainees.

Supply and Demand for Third Party Assessment

While there is a good supply of potential assessors existing in terms of people with industry experience, assessing bodies with the capabilities and resources to train individuals appropriately in assessment are currently in short supply. This gap may be filled by training provided by SSCs, or by the introduction of qualifications for assessors, as is being developed by the International Labour Organization (ILO) and NSDC; it must be recognised, however, that depending on the way that implementation of the qualification requirement occurs, a shortage of assessors may continue (for example, assessors may not be able to pay for the upgrade to their qualifications).

The challenges in estimating the volume of assessors required is complex, however. The figures are complicated by the fact that many assessors work part-time, which makes their availability difficult to predict. This data needs to be collected nationally in order to develop an accurate indication of assessment supply and demand.

Further, the need for assessments is unpredictable, with significant variations from month to month between agencies; their solution is primarily to use freelance assessors. While this ensures that a pool of assessors is on tap when required, it also raises issues of maintaining the quality of assessor skills (possibly where they are not engaged for a period of time) and also in maintaining their engagement (likely when competing with regular paid employment).

Estimates of the Skills Gap in the Assessor Workforce

The future skills assessment gap has not been forecast, as it depends upon the extent to which action is taken over current skills assessment gaps. Gaps have been estimated for illustrative purposed only. They are based on an estimate of the current gap between enrolments and assessments using the STAR data as a proxy and should note be taken as definitive figures. The calculation is based on the assumption that all learners will require assessment going forward. The assessment gap has been defined as the gap between current capacity and required capacity, i.e. the number of additional individual assessors required to enable all learners to be assessed. On this basis, skills gap across schemes can be estimated as follows:

- The total national skills assessment gap of assessors under the STAR scheme can be estimated at around 3,200.
- The skills assessment gap in Haryana is estimated to be 64 assessors.
- The skills assessment gap in Maharashtra is estimated to be 288 assessors.
- The skills assessment gap in Odisha is estimated to be 96 assessors.

Whilst these figures are illustrative only, they highlight the fact that there is currently a shortage of assessors in India, a situation that is only likely to increase as the demand for third party assessment grows as the level of training activity increases.

Funding

The payment schemes under the MES-SDI and STAR schemes are still felt by assessment agencies to be too low, even though the STAR scheme introduced a significant increase in assessment fees; across all schemes, the need to achieve volume of assessments in order to secure sufficient income is likely to cause agencies to compromise on the quality of assessments.

A number of stakeholders referred to the practice of SSCs and agencies negotiating payment splits which creates significant difficulties for smaller agencies, who are likely to have less negotiating power. Some agencies are reporting to be receiving as little as Rs.600 to complete assessments.

Geography is another key funding issue: government funded programmes overwhelmingly operate at national level and require assessors to be deployed to regions as needed; however this often causes delays in assessments as freelance assessors with the required skills are not often available at short notice in rural areas. The travel involved, and the payment for assessors, makes the funding model for many agencies untenable.

Assessment Processes

There is little evidence that assessments are reliable, valid and comparable between assessment agencies, both within the same sector and under different schemes. As assessments across the various schemes are not comparable because of their different guidelines, it is recommended that common national standards for assessment are adopted by all government funded schemes. As separate guidelines specific to the STAR scheme have been produced, it may be that these could be the basis for further guidance on assessment in the system as a whole. The introduction of the National Skills Qualifications Committee (NSQC) under the NSQF, and their future requirements for certification upon SSCs, may also address this issue. Transparency is further undermined by the lack of system-wide mechanisms for capturing information on assessment outcomes and quality across the different government funded schemes.

NSDC data and training providers involved in the STAR scheme have reported high failure rates in some sectors. Whilst this may in part be due to the rigour of the assessment process, some assessment bodies felt that the high failure rates were due in part to a lack of consistent guidance for assessors about the level at which candidates must perform and the absence of national standards for assessors. The fact that under the STAR scheme, candidates can take assessments as many times as needed, is also thought by some training providers to contribute to the high failure rate. However, it should be noted that according to NSDC data, a significant proportion of the failures were through online/IT based assessments.

Emphasis on summative assessment for certification is felt to be incorrect by many agencies, training providers and policy makers; a combined approach whereby formative coursework is also taken into consideration is felt to be a more accurate and fair way of demonstrating candidate abilities. However, the inclusion of formative assessments in the overall assessment model would require additional quality assurance measures such as the introduction of standardized assessment tools and assessment guidelines for training providers as part of an enhanced registration/affiliation system. While maintaining the necessary distance between assessment agencies and training providers that is required to ensure quality, more transparent feedback mechanisms should be encouraged between the two groups, so that mutual improvement is enabled.

The use of technology in conducting assessments is a key area of good practice, and is helping to address many issues within the assessment process, including improving the accessibility of assessments for trainees in remote areas, and reducing costs for assessment agencies. It can be argued that the use of technology for assessments and the best balance between knowledge and performance based assessment, especially in sectors that are not IT based, has not been sufficiently explored in either the MES-SDI or STAR schemes. Consequently, it is suggested that further work be done to investigate both the benefits and limitations of technology as part of a blended approach to conduct assessments on a large scale in India

Quality Assurance

The empanelment standards of the MES-SDI programme, with accreditation through the National Accreditation Board for Education and Training (NABET), were reported to have dropped significantly since the scheme began, with agencies not achieving accreditation now being permitted to remain within the scheme; recent changes to the scheme have brought quality control back under Directorate General of Employment and Training (DGET) and the Regional Directorates of Apprenticeship Training (RDATs).

In terms of empanelment requirements under the STAR scheme, all assessing bodies are pre-screened by SSCs, although the rigour of this process appears to vary between SSCs. Many SSCs only require the standard education and experience requirement; other SSCs (such as the Telecom Sector Skills Council [TSSC]; details in Appendix 2) have detailed criteria that includes applicants' recent skills training, willingness to travel for assessments, and contribution to the wider sector. The best assessment bodies have internal quality assurance processes, such as comparison of outcomes between states or the employment of external verifiers, to ensure that quality standards are met.

There also exists a potential conflict of interest in terms of quality assurance of assessment agencies by SSCs. With SSCs receiving funding from assessments completed (sometimes up to 60 per cent of the total fee), there may be limited incentive for them to investigate or 'de-panel' assessment agencies who are found to be operating below the required standard. This issue was raised by a number of the training providers interviewed, who highlighted that they rely upon SSCs to act as conduits for their feedback to assessment agencies on their performance. Despite these concerns being raised, it should be noted that under both the STAR and MES-SDI schemes, a grievance system is in place.

It was also noted that many assessors receive training of only a day from their employing agencies which is highly unlikely to produce assessors who understand the principles of assessment and their application in different sectors, levels of study and national occupational standards.

This would be addressed, however, with the introduction of qualifications in assessor skills and continual professional development requirements.

Recommendations

Skills Development, Policy and Governance

- All national and state level skills development programmes should cohere to a single set of national occupational or competency standards so that common performance standards are set
- Improved communication tools should be developed so skills bodies can more effectively share information about reforms and initiatives. These should aim to improve communication horizontally at the national level, and vertically to the states.
- A mandatory qualification for assessors should be introduced to improve the skills of assessors and the quality of assessment in India.
- Strengthened quality assurance systems should be established to monitor the processes and outcomes of assessment to ensure that the ambitious policy targets deliver quality outcomes.
- The oversight and/or regulation of SSCs should be enhanced so that assessment practices and systems across sectors are standardised and that fee structures and potential conflicts of interest can be better managed.

Supply and Demand for Third Party Assessment

- The development of systems to improve the collection of data on the supply and demand for third party assessments across government programmes should be accelerated.
- The government should consider providing public subsidies to support the phased introduction of a mandatory qualification for assessors to rapidly improve the skills of assessors.
- A mandatory program of continuous professional development for assessors should be introduced through SSCs and/or assessment bodies.
- The government should consider taking steps to ensure higher wages for assessors holding formal qualifications for assessors.

Funding

- Future funding/incentive regimes should place an equal focus on certification and placement.
- A study on the costs of assessment, separate to the costs of training, should be undertaken to identify the key variants of costs across different sectors for publicly funded provision.
- Conduct research into best practice for funding and delivering quality assessment in hard-to-reach areas.

Assessment Processes

- Clearer assessment standards should be developed to supplement the detail in NOSs and QPs to drive more consistent assessment quality across different sectors and schemes.
- Consider different options for including formative assessments in the overall assessment model for QPs, including the additional quality assurance measures required to ensure effective implementation by training providers.
- Scale up support to assessing bodies, through SSCs or other appropriate organisations, so that higher quality assessment tools can be developed and introduced.
- Ensure the existence of formal, transparent bilateral feedback mechanisms between training providers and assessing bodies.
- Undertake further research on the potential use of technology in skills assessment and how best to encourage technology adoption in the sector.

Quality Assurance

- Adopt a standard empanelment process for assessment bodies and mandate its standard usage across all SSCs and other regulatory bodies with an equivalent role.
- Consider the options to improve the accreditation/affiliation process of assessors and assessing bodies under the various schemes – including by a new or existing national regulatory body – so as to remove potential conflicts of interest and raise standards of assessment nationally.
- Continue efforts to develop national standards, career pathways and qualifications for assessors and trainers and design a national workforce development strategy for these important roles.

12

Skill Development for Unorganised Sector

Approximately 93 per cent of the country's workforce is in the unorganized sector. The sector cuts across all economic activities and includes rural and urban areas. It contributes to about 60 per cent of the country's GDP. Strengthening the skill base of the unorganized sector will improve productivity, working condition labour rights, social security and living standards. Separate institutional mechanism will be explored which will interalia plan, implement and monitor the skill development efforts for the unorganized sector. The mode of informal apprenticeship and learning will be reorganized and accommodated in the NVQF to help in horizontal and vertical mobility.

Target Groups

The target groups in the unorganized sector include own-account workers, workers and apprentices in micro enterprises; unpaid family workers; casual labourers; home-based workers; peripatetic workers and migrant labourers; out of school youth and adults in need of skills; farmers and artisans in rural areas, among others. In order to encourage participation in skill development, entry barriers such as educational qualification, transportation, loss of wages, problem of language, etc. will be suitably addressed.

Training Providers

- Various avenues/institutions including schools and public/private training institutions/civil society organizations/NGOs etc. will be encouraged to conduct skill development programmes for the unorganized sector.

- Mobile training vans will be deployed in rural and remote areas where training infrastructure is awfully deficient.
- Skill development centres will conduct skill development programmes primarily to support services and unorganized sector.
- Public training institutions will be given greater managerial and academic autonomy to design and offer programmes that meet the requirements of local economy and specific target groups.
- Flexible delivery strategy and patterns that suit the needs of the target groups, such as part/full time and on/off site training, will be adopted.
- Training will be predominantly short-term to encourage participation.
- Arrangements will be made for the testing and certification of skills acquired in non-formal and informal arrangements. These certificates will be integrated with NVQF.

Informal Apprenticeship

- Skill development programmes will be devised in existing/ traditional skills and knowledge. Mechanisms will be evolved to upgrade them into modern skill areas.
- Skills of local trainers will be upgraded in modern techniques, technologies and pedagogy. They will be trained and developed into master craftsmen. Opportunities for linking these arrangements to formal training institutions will be explored to extend expertise, pedagogical support and tools & equipment.
- Dual-type apprenticeships will be encouraged.
- Social protection mechanism for apprentices will be devised. Special efforts will be made to eliminate child labour, to improve access for girls, people with disabilities and other vulnerable groups.

Literacy and Soft Skills

Skill development initiatives for the unorganized sector will include a definite component on literacy, basic education and soft skills.

Skill Development for Self-Employment

- The focus will be given to entrepreneurship skill development for the unorganized sector.

- Institutes for entrepreneurship development, technology incubation centres and other such institutional arrangements will be utilized to support successful adoption of entrepreneurship of unorganized sector workers.

Lifelong Learning and Recognition of Prior Learning

- Competency standards and certification systems will be developed for unorganized sector work and incorporated in the national testing and certification system.
- Mechanisms will be developed for vocational counselling and career guidance;
- Information regarding employment trends and training opportunities will also be provided to motivate young people and workers to acquire and continuously upgrade their skills and knowledge.

Replication of Successful Models

Various successful models have been tried in India and around the world. In designing skill development strategies and progrmmes for the unorganized sector, successful models will be studied and adopted to suit local conditions.

13

CII Initiatives

CII played a pioneering role in the skill development movement in India, recognizing the fact that with limited natural resources and a burgeoning population. India's principal resource is its people. CII adopted a set of guiding principles for its skills initiatives:

- Capacity building while ensuring quality
- Sustainable skill development programmes
- Independent assessment and evaluation
- Focus on employability
- Global benchmarking

To take its agenda of skills development forward, CII works with divorce stakeholders such has the Government, NGOs and industry (see Fig.)

CII played a key role in the formulation of the National Skill Development Police (NSDP), announced in February 2009. The policy attempts to address the skill mismatch in the economy from the larger perspective of the vision of 'inclusive growth' illustrated in the 11th Five-Year Plan (2007-12), and proposes the establishment of a skill Development Initiative (SDI). The initiative '...will empower all individuals through improved skills, knowledge, nationally and internationally recognized qualifications to gain access to decent employment and ensure India's competiveness in the global market'.

To bring about a paradigm shift a National Skill Development Mission was announced and the Union Cabinet approved a 'Coordinated Action Plan of Skill Development' envisaging a target of 500 million skilled persons by the year 2022. A three-tier institutional structure was set up namely:

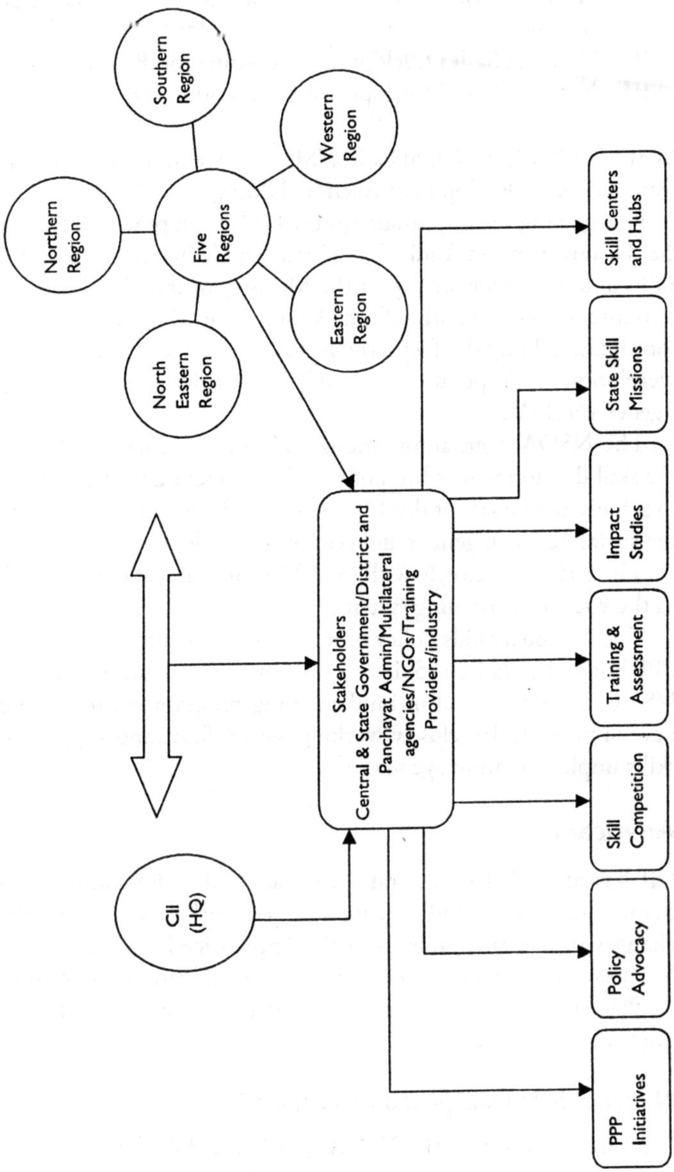
CII
(HQ)
Stakeholders
Central & State Government/District and
Panchayat Admin/Multilateral
agencies/NGOs/Training
Providers/industry
Five
Regions
Northern
Region
Southern
Region
Western
Region
Eastern
Region
North
Eastern
Region
PPP
Initiatives
Policy
Advocacy
Skill
Competition
Training &
Assessment
Impact
Studies
State Skill
Missions
Skill Centers
and Hubs

I. Prime Minister's National Council on the Skill Development (NCSD);
II. National Skill Development Coordination Board (NSDCB)
III. National Skill Development Corporation (NSDC)

As of May 2013, the NCSD and NSDCB have been subsumed into the National Skill Development Agency (NSDA).

Recognizing the importance of the skill development in the country, the Government of India has created a dedicated Department for Skills and Entrepreneurship in the Ministry of the Skill Development, Entrepreneurship, Youth Affairs & Sports in May 2014. As a central coordinating body the Department has the charge of the National Skill Development Corporation (NSDC) and National Skill Development Agency (NSDA).

The NSDA is an autonomous body to coordinate and harmonize the skill development efforts of the Government and the private sector to achieve the targets of the 12th Five-Year Plan and beyond and bridge the social, regional gender and economic divide.

The CII works closely with the NSDA to bring about policy changes in the vocational training system.

The National Skills Policy brought about the formation of an unique PPP body, the National Skills Development Corporation (NSDC). The NSDC is instrumental in implementing programmes to enhance skill development. CII is closely working with NSDC and supporting their skills implementation agenda.

Advocacy

CII has identified issues and gaps that need to be addressed to meet the requirements of industry for a skilled workforce and has advocated changes in the Amendments in the Apprenticeship Act. A special case has been advocated for a single uniform qualification framework.

Platforms for advocacy are created through Conferences and Summits.

National Skill Qualification Framework

Working closely with the NSDA, CII has had deliberations on a wide range of issues with its members on the need for a National Skill Qualification. Framework (NSQF). The NSQF is a framework that classifies qualifications according to levels of knowledge along with skills.

Qualifications are made up of occupational standards for specific areas of learning units. This will provide the stakeholders such as learners, education and skill training providers and employers an opportunity to gain equivalence of qualifications across specific skill sectors.

Conferences

National Conferences on Skill Development

The National Conference on Skill Development is a unique platform where issues of national importance are highlighted and deliberated with the aim of brining out plausible recommendations to strengthen the skills ecosystem.

Global Summit on Skili Development

In order to ensure quality with quantity, it is necessary to benchmark the skills of our country with the developed skills ecosystem. The Global Summit on Skill Development, a biennial event, witnesses one of the largest congregation of skill providers. The objective is to align the national framework with the international best practices.

Skill Development Programmes Under Public Private Partnerships

Led by a belief in the value of partnerships to catalyse skills development, CII entered into the Public Private Partnership space with the Ministry of Labour and Employment through the flagship schemes 'Upgradation of 1396 Industrial Training Institutes (ITIs) through Public Private Partnership (PPP)' and the Modular Employable Skills schemes (MES).

The ITIs represent the formal vocational training system in India Recognizing the need to enable ITIs to effectively respond to market demand, in 2007, the Ministry of Labour and Employment launched the PPP upgradation scheme. The industry participated actively, with CII Member adopting 390 ITIs. This PPP has enabled industry-led development through curriculum building and Training of Trainers. An impact study has been conducted to understand successful replicable models.

The Modular Employable Skills (MES) scheme aims at providing vocational training to school leavers, existing workers, and ITIs graduates, etc. to improve their employability by optimally using the existing infrastructure available in Government, private institutions, and industry. Existing skills can be tested and certified under this scheme which primary aims at developing competency standards, course curricula, learning material, and assessment standards in the country.

As a National Assessing Body in the Modular Employable Skills (MES) scheme, CII has built a qualitative assessor base.

CII National Skill Development Corporation

A unique one of its kind, Public Partnership, the National Skill Development Corporation (NSDC) has been formed to narrow the existing gap between demand and supply of skilled labour force in the country. CII is on the board of NSDC and both organizations believe that for inclusive growth a sectoral approach is the key.

Sector Skills Councils

CII facilities the creation of 'sector bodies' within industry, and supports the NSDC through the Sector Skills Councils (SSCs), which are industry-led bodies to ensure a demand driven vocational training system. CII has facilitated the formation of Sector Skill Councils in Healthcare, Logistics, Banking, Financial Services and Insurance (BFSI) with Bombay Stock Exchange, Life Sciences, Beauty & Wellness and Hospitality. Additional SSCs in the high growth sectors are in process.

World Skills International Competitions

The biennial Worldskills International Competitions led by National Skill Development Corporation (NSDC) starting 2010 is a platform to benchmark youth to global standards.

Earlier, CII represented India in the World skills International Competitions from 2007-2010, It embarked on this initiative with the twin objective of putting India on the global skill map while encouraging competitiveness within the country.

Since 2010, CII has been working closely with the NSDC to select and train competitors in manufacturing and services trades for the upcoming International competitions.

Private industry has supported this journey by building teams of world standards which will ultimately add to the pool of highly skilled resources.

Capacity Building and Employability

CII has been working actively to build capacity and increase employability of people through various outreach programmes.

Outreach Programmes

CII engages closely with state and district level administration, multilateral agencies, public sector undertakings, non-state actors and skill development missions to enable skill training to the marginalized sections of society thus ensuring an employable workforce.

Training of Trainers

Recruiting capable trainers is an essential part of improving quality CII, in consultation with the State Governments is imparting training of Trainer programmes. The focus is on upgrading the skills of existing trainers and building capacity of new trainers to meet the shortage in demand. About 4-5 training programmes in a year are conducted across the four regions within India.

Job Fairs for ITI Graduates

With the objective of connecting employers and youth from ITIs to industry, CII organizes job fairs across India. This provides jobs to ITI graduates while enabling access for employers to a talent pool.

Professional Skills Development for Undergraduate Students

An initiatives of CII National Committee on Skill Development for developing and running short-term courses for students of the University of Delhi.

The objective is to work for a socially relevant cause by imparting job relevant employability skills to students of DU during their term in University and at the same time addressing the skill shortages faced by Indian industry.

Skill Hubs and Skill Gurukuls

Collaborating with the State Government and the private sector, CII has set up Skill Hubs and Skill Gurukuls in remote districts of India, which impact training in various skills.

Large Skill Centers/Hubs with capacity of 1500-5000 beneficiaries per annum have been set up at:

Chhindwara (Madhya Pradesh) – a unique partnership with 9 industry members

Bhiwadi (Rajesthan) – a multi skill center with focus on manufacturing trades

Balasore (Odisha) – a multi skill center with focus on service trades

An important aspect of the unorganized sector training programme is the focus on short-duration modules of local relevance for encouraging greater participation. A similar aspect will be the emphasis on self employment.

Rural Skill Gurukuls

Through the skill gurukuls, CII reaches out to marginalised youth at the district level and attempts to provide technical education and hands-on training.

The skill Gurukuls are vocational finishing schools with fulltime, residential training of 30-45 days in trades such as weiding, construction, catering, driving with a practical orientation. It is a one-of-its-kind self-sustainable model with zero-subsidity for blue collar trades by giving 100 percent micro finance assistance funding by NABARD. There is 100 percent placement assurance due to upfront tie up with CII members.

Other Outreach Programmes

HPCL Swavalamban Project for training below poverty line youth leading to employment/self-employment is being successfully implemented in 17 states through 25 centers. Through this HPCL's CSR initiatives, with CII as an implementation partner, a large number of BPL youth, with focus on women, PWDs, SC & STs, have been trained leading to employment/self-employment.

CII supported by the European Union and in partnership with British Council, City & Guilds and Aditya Birla Group is implementing a model initiative in 2 backward districts for training marginalized youth in Agricultural, Hospitality and Auto servicing & maintenance trades as well as soft skills training and linking to employment/self employment. This is being replicated in other districts in India.

Understanding the need for on ground intervention, CII is working in J&K as well as the North-East for training marginalized youth and facilitating employment self-employment.

Under "Project Happy Landing", CII is working with the Indian Air Force to give industry linked training to retiring air warriors and linking them to employment.

Competitions

To promote vocational training and encourage competitiveness among the youth, CII has been actively involved in institutionalizing competitions.

The CII Work Skills Competitions has been recognized as a robust worker management relationship building tool.

The World Skills International Competitions are a pathway to benchmark the skills of the country to developed skill ecosystems.

WorkSkills Competition

The Workskills competition was initiated by CII on the lines of the skills Olympics organized by the industry in Europe as a means of promoting vocational training in industrial skills. The first CII workskills Competition was held in 1989 at Advanced Training Institute, Dasnagar, Howrah, where Over 200 workers from the Indian Industry participated.

Encouraged by the overwhelming response received in the first WorkSkills Competition, CII institutionalized this competition as a major event for the industrial workforce. The competition has completed 25 years. The winners in the below 22 years category are possible competitors for the WorldSkills International Competitions.

WorldSkills International Competition

The CII had played a lead role in placing India on the World Skills map. The competition regarded as the 'Olympic of skills' showcases the pinnacle of excellence in vocational training.

CII represented India in the WorldSkills International Competitions:

- Japan 2007 – Indian contingent participated for the first time
- Calgary, Canada 2009 – An Indian participant from Geedee Technical Training Institute (GTTI), Coimbatore won the Silver Medal in mould making
- London 2011 – 7 competitors in 5 trades participated along with a CII skills delegation comprising of officials from Government and private sector.

- First Indian Business delegation to WorldSkills London 2013
- Germany 2013 – Indian competitors participated in the trades of (I) Mechatronics (II) CNC Milling (III) CNC Turning (IV) welding (V) Electronics (VI) Plastic Die Engineering

CII believes that Industry will invest in skill development in its own interest and is working in partnership with industry and Government to meet the goal of 500 million skilled workforce by 2022.

14

A Common Framework for Skills Development

Meeting Today's and Tomorrow's Skills Needs

International experience shows that countries that have succeeded in linking skills development to gains in productivity, employment and development have targeted skills development policy towards three main objectives:

- matching supply to current demand for skills;
- helping workers and enterprises adjust to change; and
- building and sustaining competencies for future labour market needs.

The first objective is about the relevance and quality of training. Matching the provision of skills with labour market demand requires labour market information systems to generate, analyse and disseminate reliable sectoral and occupational information systems to generate, analyse and disseminate reliable sectoral and occupational information, and institutions that connect employers with training providers. It is also about equality of opportunity in access to education, training, employment services and employment, in order that the demand for training from all sectors of society is met.

The second objective is about easing the movement of workers and enterprises from declining or low-productivity activities and sectors into expanding and higher-productivity activities and sectors. Learning new skills, upgrading existing ones and lifelong learning can all help workers to maintain their employability and enterprises to adapt and remain competitive.

The third objectives calls for a long-term perspective, anticipating the skills that will be needed in the future and engendering a virtuous circle in which more and better education and training fuels innovation, investment, technological change, economic diversification and competitiveness, and thus job growth.

A Holistic Approach

At its 97th Session in 2008 the International Labour Conference called for a holistic approach to skills development encompassing the following features:

1. continuous and seamless pathways of learning, starting with pre-school and primary education that adequately prepares young people for secondary and higher education and vocational training, going on to provide career guidance, labour market information and counselling as young women and men move into the labour market, and offering workers and entrepreneurs opportunities for continuous learning to upgrade their competencies and learn new skills throughout their lives;
2. development of core skills- including literacy, numeracy, communication skills, teamwork, problem-solving skills and learning ability- which, along with awareness of workers' rights and an understanding of entrepreneurship, are not linked to performance in specific occupations but from the building blocks for lifelong learning and adaptability to change;
3. development of higher-level skills-professional, technical and human resource skills-enabling workers to profit from or create opportunities for high-quality and/or high-wage jobs;
4. portability of skills, based first on core skills, so that workers can apply their existing knowledge and experience to new occupations or industries, and second on systems that codify, standardize, assess and certify skills, so that levels of competence can be easily recognized by social partners in different labour sectors across national, regional or international labour markets; and
5. employability (for wage work or self-employment), which results from all these factors-a foundation composed of core

skills, access to education, availability of training opportunities, motivation, ability to take advantage of opportunities for continuous learning and support in doing so, and recognition of acquired skills.

A Life-cycle Perspective

Skills development can fruitfully be viewed from a life-cycle perspective of building, maintaining and improving skills. Policy interventions need to be designed accordingly. The essential stages can be summarized as follows:

- *Children:* building important foundation skills through early childhood and initial education, keeping in mind that the benefits of these investments will be reaped in the longer term.
- *Young people:* consolidating foundation skills and gaining important workplace skills and experience for a successful transition from school to work.
- *Mature and older workers:* maintaining and upgrading existing skills and gaining new skills while also certifying the skills and competencies acquired in the working life.

It is also important to recognize that skills build upon on another, and that acquiring foundation skills in literacy and numeracy, as well as "learning to learn", are absolutely essential for acquiring further skills and competencies.

Given the inevitable limitations on resources, difficult trade-offs will need to be made between different policy objectives in determining priorities in public investments skills development.

Convergence Across Policies

Skills and employment policies should be viewed together. The full value of one policy set is realized when it supports the objectives of the other.

One of the main challenges of public policy is to foster institutional arrangements through which government departments, employers, workers and training needs, institutions can effectively respond to changing skill and training needs and indeed play a strategic and forward-looking role in anticipating future needs. For investments in training to yield maximum benefit to workers, enterprises and economies, countries' capacity for coordination is most important in three areas:

1. connecting basic education to technical training, technical training to labour market entry, and labour market entry to workplace and lifelong learning;
2. ensuring continuous communication between employers and training providers so that training meets the needs and aspirations of workers and enterprises; and
3. integrating skills development policies with other policy areas-not only labour market and social protection policies, but also industrial, investment, trade and technology policies, and regional or local development policies.

Countries use a variety of coordination mechanisms: national inter-ministerial bodies; sector-based bodies bringing together training institutions and providers with employers' and workers' representatives; and decentralized local bodies. These mechanisms involve substantial investments of time and money, and they work when, and only when, all stakeholders can see their own objectives supported by others. For example:

- line ministries responsible for public infrastructure, research and innovation, environmental protection, international competitiveness and regional integration-to name just a few – rely on a skilled workforce;
- employers seek a well-trained workforce capable of further learning so that their enterprises can take advantage of new technologies and adapt to changing market conditions; and
- workers and their trade unions know that time spent acquiring skills leads to better employment and standards of living.

In sum, the effective utilization of skills in the workplace both depends on and contributes to conditions conductive to innovation and enterprise development; effective labour market orientation and mediation services; and well-informed decisions abour education and training policies.

15

Demand and Supply Dynamics

The average age of India's population by 2020 is projected to be the lowest in the world- around 29 years compared to 37 years in China and the United States of America, 45 years in West Europe, and 48 years in Japan. While the global economy is expected to witness a shortage of young population of around 56 million by 2020, India will be the only country with a youth surplus of 47 million. India's demographic transition makes it imperative to ensure employment opportunities for millions of youth each year. Alongside employment, skill development is equally important as over the years jobs have become more skill-intensive with changes in technology as well as increased inter-linkages across economic activities.

The skill development issue in India is pertinent both at the demand and supply level. Generating employment is definitely a challenge given the enormity of population entering workface each year. From the supply side, the issue is primarily related to employability of the workface due to varying reasons ranging from poor education, lack of training facilities, inadequate skilling, quality issues leading to mismatch of skill requirements, and poor perception of vocational skilling vis-à-vis formal education. These have inadvertently created skill shortage and also contributed to higher unemployment. Hence, both employment and employability are key factors of concern today. The magnitude of the problem can be gauged from some of the statistics detailed below.

Literacy Levels in India are Extremely Low

As per the twelfth plan document 55 per cent of workforce has education only up to primary level. School dropout rate is also high, with 19.8

per cent dropping out after class V, additional 16.5 per cent dropping out after class VIII and future 11.1 per cent dropping out after class X.

Formally Skilled Workforce is Less than 3 Per Cent of Total Workforce

Unfortunately, the current size of India's formally skilled workforce is very small. Only 6.8 percent of persons aged 15 years and above have received or were receiving vocational training, of which only 2.8 percent was through formal channels while 4 percent was through the informal system. In contrast, skilled workforce in other countries is much higher – Korea (96 per cent), Germany (75 per cent), Japan (80 per cent) and United Kingdom (68 per cent).

School Dropout Rate in India

Class	*Dropout Rate*
I–V	19.8
I–VIII	36.3
I–X	47.4

Source: Ministry of HRD

Share of Population (15 Years & Above) Receiving Vocational Training (in per cent)

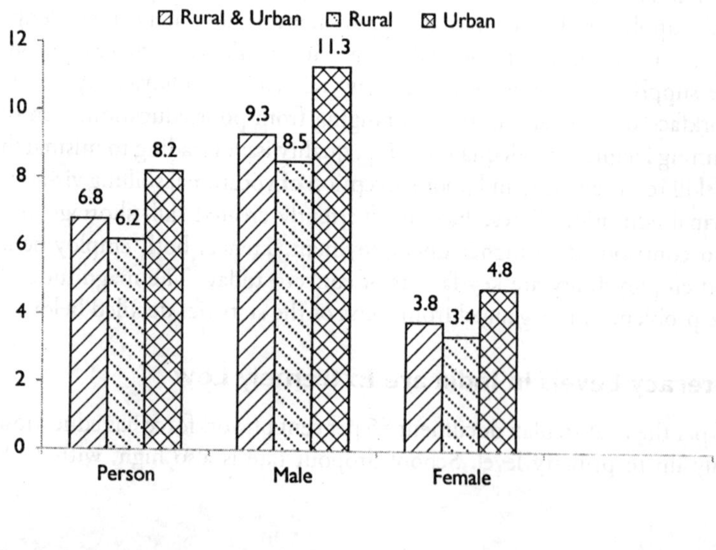

Poor Literacy Levels Impede Skilling through Formal Channels

Amongst the formally skilled labour force, 74 have higher secondary or higher education levels, and amongst the labour force with informal skills, 78 per cent of the workforce has completed only middle or lower education. Such skewed nature of skilling can be attributed to two factors – a) the education level entry requirements in the current skill set-up makes it difficult for workers with minimal education to access formal skills training; and b) lack of education also impedes the ability to absorb higher level of skills.

Inadequate Training Capacities

The number of people who enter the work force age group every year is estimated to be 26 million. With average labour participation rate of 90 per cent for male and 30 per cent for female, at least 16.16 million will enter the workforce and would need to acquire skills. However, current annual skilling capacity, including training for the farm sector, in India is estimated at only 7 million. The table below highlights the dismal state of training capacities at the ITIs, which are a key source of skill training in India. Enrolments in vocational training are way below the enrolments in formal education. As against the enrolment of 23.76 million students in higher education, the skill training capacities in it is is mere 1.69 million. Training partners of NSDC have collectively trained 3.4 million youths in 2015-16.

Unemployment amongst Higher Education is Also High

The Labour Bureau's survey report for 2013-14 reveals that the propotion of unemployment in labour force with higher education levels is also high. Amongst 9 per cent of the graduates and post graduate labour force is currently unemployed as against less than 1 per cent in case of illiterates and semi-literate labour force. Besides the issue of

No. of ITIs with Total Seating Capacity

No. of Govt. ITIs	*No. of Private. ITIs*	*Total ITIs*	*Total Seating Capacity of ITIs*
2284	9680	11964	1692836

Source: Ministry of Labour and Employment

Table 4: Enrolment in Higher Education in India

Level	*Enrolment in University Departments/Colleges*	*Enrolment in Affiliated Colleges*	*Total*	*% Share*
Graduate	2125.559	18,104,033	20,2295,92	85.12
Post Graduate	774.557	2,160,432	2,934,989	12.35
Research	156.845	43,885	200,730	0.85
Diploma/Certificate	156.909	242,740	399,649	1.68
Grande Total	3.213.870	20,551,090	23,764,960	100

Source: UGC Annual Report, 2013-14

unemployment, this data also points towards the issue of employability due to mismatch of skills with the work requirements.

Amongst the formally trained labour force, the unemployment rate is above 10 per cent for several trades and is significantly high in case of "engineering trades other than civil and computer trades' (25.2 per cent) and 'textile related work' (16.7 per cent). Amongst the informally trained workforce, the percentage of unemployed is mostly low (below 5 per cent) for most of the trades except for certain trades like fitter (10.7 per cent) and 'engineering trades other than civil and computer trades' (12.2 per cent).

Employability Levels are Very Low

The extent of employability gap can also be gauged from the 2014 survey report (National Employability Report 2014) by Aspiring Minds, which shows that out of the six hundred thousand engineers that graduate annually, only 18.43 per cent are employable for the Software Engineer-IT service role, while a dismal 3.95 per cent are appropriately trained to be directly deployed on projects. For core jobs in mechanical, electronics/electrical and civil engineering only a mere 7.49 per cent are employable. As per the report, the key reason behind such poor employability statistics is inadequate preparation in the domain area, i.e. the ability to apply basis principles of say, computer engineering or mechanical engineering to real world problems.

16

Quality and Relevance

Quality and relevance of skill development are key to India's global competiveness as well as improving an individual's access to decent employment. For enterprises to complete in the global economy, the quality of training must reach world standards and be relevant to the needs of national and international markets.

To increase the relevance with feature employment market including promotion of self employment, soft skills and entrepreneurship skills will be made integral part of skill development.

The demographic advantage that the country enjoys, coupled with prospects of global storages in skill as the world population ages, means that the country could be supplying skills to the world.

Quality Assurance is based on five key functions:

- Validation of Qualification for ensuring that qualification reflect market needs and workplace requirements and are expressed in the form of competencies with clear assessment criteria;
- Validation of Training Process for ensuring that paper tools, techniques, methodologies and material, as suggested in the curriculum/standards are used by the resource persons;
- Quality Assured Assessment of Learners for ensuring that assessment is based on national standards (competencies) and uses valid and reliable assessment methods;
- Accreditation of Training Providers and Training Institutions for ensuring that training is delivered by competent and qualified trainers in well-resourced and managed institutions;

- Research and information for linking the supply of skilled workers to trends in well-researched Labour Market Information (LMI) covering both the organized and unorganized sectors of the economy;

The objective of enforcing quality and relevance in skill development will be realize through improving infrastructure, improving quality of trainer and developing National Vocation Qualification Framework.

Quality of Infrastructure

Extensive use of information & Communication Technology will be promoted for learning or increasing the impact of learning.

Optimum use of existing physical infrastructure will be ensured in multiple shifts or otherwise.

Industries will be encourager to provide their spare capacity to supplements skill development activities.

Physical infrastructure will be created, expanded and upgraded according to skill requirements of specific sectors of economy.

Quality of Trainer

Innovative ways of recruiting trainers will be adopted including the employment of former trainees who have gained workplace experience and of practitioners of a craft, trained as master craft persons.

Innovative skill development schemes, in which trainees acquire theoretical learning at the institutions while obtaining practical skills in the workplace, will be devised.

Retired employees mainly from defense will be retrained to meet the requirement of trainers.

Award and incentive mechanism, include reward and career progression systems, will be reviewed and institutionalized to improve the status of trainers.

A system of granting Accredited Trainer Status for a limited period, to all vocational trainers of programmes, leading to National Vocational qualifications will be developed.

Special efforts will be made to improve the gender balance among trainers.

National Vocational Qualifications Framework

To stimulate and support reforms in skills development and to facilitate nationally standardized and acceptable, international comparability of qualifications, a "National Vocational Qualification Framework" will be established. All the existing Institutions/Councils/Boards under different Ministries, involved in skill development will be encouraged to follow National Vocational Qualification Framework.

This framework will have the following features:

- Competency based qualifications and certification on the basis of nationally agreed standards and criteria;
- Certification for learning achievement and qualification;
- A range of national qualification levels – based on criteria with respect to responsibility, complexity of activities, and transferability of competencies;
- The avoidance of duplication and overlapping of qualifications while assuring the inclusion of all training needs;
- Modular character where achievements can be made in small steps and accumulated for gaining recognizable qualification;
- Quality Assurance regime that would promote the portability of skill and labour market mobility;
- Lifelong learning through an improved skill recognition system; recognition of prior learning whether in formal, non-formal or informal arrangements;
- Open the flexible system which will permit competent individuals to accumulate their knowledge and skill through testing & certification into higher diploma and degree;
- Different learning pathways – academic and vocational – that integrate formal and non-formal learning, notably learning in the workplace, and that offer vertical mobility from vocational to academic learning;
- Guidance for individuals in their choice of training and career planning;
- Compatibility of general educational and qualifications at appropriate levels;
- Nationally agreed framework of affiliation and accreditation of institutions.
- Multiple certification agencies/institutions will be encouraged within NVQF.

17

Equity and Access

Equal access to skill development is essential for all social groups particularly women and disadvantages section of society, to help them in securing decent employment and moving out of poverty. Removing barriers to access and addressing their specific needs are key elements in achieving inclusive growth.

Entry barriers such as education qualification, transportation, loss of wages, language etc. will be addressed. While enhancing the opportunity of skill development for all, entry assessments will be developed to channelize people with different profiles and needs into appropriate skill development programmes. The efforts will be combined with a major initiative in raising awareness among the target groups about the benefit of skill development, employment and learning opportunities and also about support schemes that enable them to participate in training. In addition to vocational skills, the provision of soft (or Life) skills – including basic literacy, numeracy, occupational safety and health, hygiene, basic labour rights, team work and confidence building – will be made as an integral component of the curricula. This will also help in empowerment of vulnerable groups.

Vocational Training for Women

Skill development for employability will be used as an agent of change in promoting women's employment. Women face a multitude of barriers in accessing skills and productive employment, remaining on the job due to effect of globalization or otherwise and advancing to higher level jobs, as well as returning to the labour market after a period of absence spent, for example, in raising children.

A policy of non-discrimination will be pursued vigorously to provide equal access for women to skill development and employment. This policy will aim to raise women's participation to at least 30 per cent. Proactive measures that overcome barriers and facilitate participation, such as hostels for women, scholarships, transport, training materials and loans, will be made available on a large scale. The Women's Vocational Training Programme will be expanded and the institutional network providing training facilities exclusively for women, so that they can obtain skills with high wage and self-employment potential will be greatly expanded. In order to promote skills and employability of women, the sectors which employ a large number of women will be identified. These may include construction, home-based traditional crafts or piece rate work, financial and health service as well as agricultural sectors. Gender stereotyping in vocational courses will be eliminated to encourage women's participation in non-traditional occupations, including existing and emerging technological fields.

Rural, Border, Hilly and Difficult Areas and Regional Imbalance in Opportunities

Infrastructure and programmes for skill development are particularly scarce in rural and difficult areas and thus the problem of access to training is most acute in these areas. Specially the women are increasingly the main workers in rural households, as their husbands migrate but often equipped with only traditional and outdated skills and knowledge. Skill development in rural areas contributes to improve productivity and working conditions in the agricultural sector while at the same time enabling rural workers, particularly young people to access emerging employment opportunities beyond the agricultural sector enable. In view of the limited training infrastructure, a range of infrastructure facilities, including schools, community centres and local government buildings, will be utilized as training venues. Institute for entrepreneurship training such as Rural Development & Self-employment Training Institutes (RUDSETI) will be further promoted. The Government itself will set up public institutions and will also promote the establishment of private sector training institutions through a package of suitable designed incentives such as provision of land and financial assistance.The convergence with national employment programmes, such as National Rural Employment Guaranteed Scheme (NREGS), will be promoted as an opportunity for imparting skills training in rural areas. Training facilities need to be updated regularly so as to meet changing demands. Village- or block-based skill development centres will be set up to serve the needs of local communities. Facilitated by the district officers and panchayats, these skill development centres will play a pivotal role in identifying local employment opportunities and providing, or organizing, adequate training and post-training support according to the specific needs of local areas. The centres will also function as information centres for training and employment opportunities as well as various support schemes. This effort will be combined with the creation of incentive mechanisms in motivating, particularly youth to participate in training and removal of other barriers in accessing training. Various mobile training arrangements will be deployed to reach out to remote and difficult areas. Skill development for self-employment will be an important component in these skill development efforts in rural areas. Post-training support, including mentoring for access to markets, credit and appropriate technologies, is an important part of skill development strategy for self-employment. Training modules will incorporate specific needs of target groups, e.g. literacy, the level of education and the local language. The delivery of training will be flexible in terms of hours and duration to encourage participation, particularly among women. In general there is a regional imbalance in training opportunities and some parts of the country are quite deficient in skill development institutions. In order to provide more equitable access across the country, special efforts will be mounted to establish training facilities in deficient regions.

Disadvantaged Groups: Scheduled Castes, Scheduled Tribes, Other Backward Classes

The reservation applicable to these groups will be strictly enforced with appropriate gender composition. Existing schemes for benefiting these groups will be reviewed, strengthened and made more effective. Efforts will be made to mobilize capabilities and expertise of civil society organizations. New innovative schemes and measures will also be devised to ensure full and effective participation by these groups, as well as the accrual of real benefits from skill development initiatives.

Minorities

Skill development opportunities for minorities groups will be expanded, particularly in Minority Concentrated Areas (MCAs). Existing schemes benefiting these groups will be reviewed, strengthened and made more effective. Efforts will be made to mobilize capabilities and expertise of civil society organizations. Formalization of non-formal skill acquisition and transfer will also be promoted in traditional art and craft sectors.

Persons with Disabilities

The current level of participation of persons with disabilities in skill programmes is very low, despite guidelines of reserving 3 per cent of the seats for them. The guidelines apply only to the government sector. People with varying degrees of physical and mental disabilities will be provided with appropriate adjustment training and skills training to bring them in the economic mainstream and make them productive citizens. This Policy aims to expand the facilities for people with disabilities and to provide reasonable accommodation that enables them to access the facilities through suitable transport and building designs. The number of Vocational Rehabilitation Centres will be doubled and expanded further in subsequent Plans Similar efforts will also be made at the State level to improve access and outreach. Training will be integrated with efforts to secure appropriate employment opportunities. Programmes of public awareness and community participation will be strengthened to promote demand for vocational training by people with disabilities as well as to facilitate their inclusion in the labour market.

School Drop-Outs and Child Labour

School education would be strengthened to reduce the school dropouts. The quality of school education will influence the effectiveness of skill development programme as a whole. This will lay solid foundation for young people to acquire employable skills and engage in continuous skill upgradetion throughout their working life. School education will be used as a tool to increase vocational awareness among the young people. School drop-outs (leaving the schools before completing XII standards), child labour and out-of-school youth need to be given alternative education coupled with skill development opportunities to bring them into the economic and social mainstream. Short term market oriented, demand-driven programmes will provide a flexible delivery framework suited to the characteristics and circumstance of the target group. Multi-skilling Multi-entry and exit, and linkages to skill upgradation opportunities in the future, will characterize such programmes. The scheme of Modular Employable Skills (i.e. short-term employable skills) will be expanded greatly to cater to the large size of the group. Formal education requirements in accessing training will be reviewed in order to facilitate easy access.

Economically Challenged Persons below Poverty Line

Skill development for employability is an important strategy in the fight against poverty. Accordingly, the poor will have a priority claim and easy access to opportunities for skill development. Efforts will be made to mitigate the impact of these economic barriers at different stages, as well as actively promote access of the poor to educational and skill development opportunities through specially designed schemes and measures. Such measures as special coaching for competing in admission tests, provision of non-formal skill development opportunities and the expanded provisions of scholarships, books and soft-loans will be developed and implemented.

18

Public-Private Partnership

Skill development initiatives in India traditional have been led by the government with the establishment of the Industrial Training Institutes (ITAs) in the early years of post-independent India to provide skilled manpower for meeting the needs of the country's fiedgling industrial sector. Initially, they were run by the central government, but in the 1960s, they were transferred to the states. Over the years, in addition to the government-run ITIs, a number of private sector-run Industrial Training Centres (ITCs) were also allowed to set up. Since then, the ITIs and ITCs have grown in numbers with numerous vocational courses being added to cater to the changing needs of industry. Curriculum too, has been changed at periodical interval to ensure that these facilities continued to be relevant for the private sector.

At the beginning of the last decade, however, many stakeholders had already started asking questions whether the ITIs and ITCs – as they were organized and run then – should be restructured with the help of the private sector to preserve their existence and meet the objectives, for which they were established, in the first place, even in post-reform India.

The First Experiments

Conscious of the need to involve the private sector in the modernization of the ITIs, the government in the early 2000s decided to embrace the concepts of public-private partnership in the ITIs, with the necessity for the PPP approach emphasized by the Prime Minister at an award function of the Ministry of Labour and Employment in New Delhi on October 4, 2004.

Subsequently, out of 1,896 ITIs during the financial year 2005-2006 (April 01, 2005 to March 31, 2006), it was decided to upgrade100 ITIs through domestic resources, 400 ITIs with World Bank assistance and significantly, the remaining 1,396 through the PPP mode.

The scheme 'Upgradation of 1,396 Government ITIs through Public-Private Partnership' was launched in 2007-2008. Under this scheme, one industry partner is associated with each ITI to lead the process of upgradation. An Institute Management Committee (IMC) is contributed or reconstituted with the industry partner or its representative as chairperson and registered as a society. An interest free loan of $0.5 million is given directly to the Chairman of the IMC for upgrading training infrastructure. After keeping a certain amount as seed money (maximum up to 50 per cent of the loan), the balance is planned to be utilized within a period of 5 years from the year of release.

Financial and academic autonomy is granted to manage the affairs of the ITI. State governments continue to have ownership of the institute and regulate the fees, and admission, except for 20 per cent of the seats which are delegated to the management. A memorandum of understanding is signed among different stakeholders. Till September 2009, 721 ITIs had been covered under this scheme.

In May 2007, the government also made operational the Modular Employability Scheme (MES) under its Skill Development Initiative Scheme (SDI) to further the PPP agenda. SDI is a 5-year project during which one million persons are proposed to be trained and the existing skills are to be tested and certified. The objective of the scheme is to provide employable skills to school leavers, existing workers and ITI/ITC graduates to improve their employability by optimally utilizing the infrastructure available in government, private institutions and industry. Skill levels of persons already employed can also be tested and certified under this scheme.

Public-private partnership is envisaged in the form of active participation of the industry/private sector in every stage of design and implementation of the scheme:

- Forecasting of emerging areas of employment at micro level
- Development of course curricula of various trades
- Development of instructional material for training
- Assist in the training of trainers, whenever required
- Making available their training and testing facilities, wherever required
- Provide on-the-job training in their establishments

- Development of assessment standards
- Monitoring and quality assurance
- Assistance in placement of graduates
- Providing trade experts to work as assessors of competencies
- Voluntary donation of equipment to the ITIs/other training institutions
- Providing guest faculty in new trades

In parallel, to address needs of sectors, different ministries, such as Ministry of Textile and Tourism, launched their own version of PPP projects. Also Ministry of Rural Development as well as Ministry of Housing and Poverty Alleviation announced scheme of livelihood, by inviting the private sector to provide skill-based initiatives. Over a period time, multiple ministries had a variety of programmes, some run by the centre and other in partnership with the states Simultaneously, the states also started skill development programmes in the PPP mode as well. However, there was a felt need to increase capacity, align and coordinate the programmes and also focus on outcomes. State government in India has also taken PPP road. For example, Karnataka State has collaborated with Kangan University of Australia and TAFE Vocational Education Institution for training programme for trainers, and Tamil Nadu State Government has established vocational training institute in PPP model in sectors like aviation and shipping.

Unlocking the Potential of Private Sector (2008–09)

In August 2008, the Prime Minister outlined his vision for skill development in India. He started that 'experts have estimated that India has the Capacity to create 500 million certified and skilled technicians by the year 2022'.

The Prime Minister also outlined the institutional structure at the national level for coordinated action in the skills apace. This consisted of the establishment of a National Council for Skill Development. Chaired by the Prime Minister himself, at the apex to lay down the board framework for this arena, a National Skill Development Corporation Board (NSDCB) coordinated by the Planning Commission to combine public and private prongs of action and the setting up of a National Skill Development Corporation (NSDC) as a no-profit-no-loss company through the public-private partnership route to catalyse private sector involvement in the skills apace.

In March 2009, the government announced a National Policy on Skill Development laying down the framework within which it wanted skills-related training to be conducted. The policy clarified the role that different stakeholders – government, industry, trade union and civil society – would need to play for the creation of a skills ecosystem in India.

Making a departure from the past, the 2009 Skill Development Policy clearly specified that skill-related training should become out come focused and linked to jobs and employability. It said that skills should allow for a seamless transfer form a vocational education stream to a formal education system.

The Policy said that the government should complement private sector initiatives in skill development and emphasized the need for short-term, industry-relevant courses. Significantly, the policy also talked of encouraging innovation in delivery and more public-private partnership in the skills space.

NSDC Transforming the Skills Landscape

A unique experiment in the skills arena, NSDC was officially launched in October 2009 with a mandate to skill 150 million people by 2022 in 20 high growth sectors and unorganized sectors identified by the government and the informal segment through a three-pronged approach revolving around creating, funding and enabling sustainable skills training initiatives in the private space.

Structured as a PPP with government ownership restricted to 49 per cent of the equity capital, majority ownership of the NSDC rests with the private sector with the shareholdings equally dispersed among 3 National Industry Associations/Chambers of Commerce and 7 sector-specific industry organizations. The funds for meeting the funding requirements, through, are made available to the NSDC through a trust called the National Skill Development Fund (NSDF). NSDC acts as an Investment manager for the NSDF, whose corpus of $330 million has gone up to $550 million following the Finance Minister's announcement of a further infusion of $220 million in 2012-2013. Going forward, the NSDF is envisaged to attract bilateral, multilateral and private funding.

A not-for-profit NSDC is a board-managed enterprise, with its 16 directors (6 from the government and 12 seats held by private sector Shareholders) taking the final call on how best to structure the funding and which proposals should be financially supported by the organization.

Over the nearly two-and-a-half years that the NSDC has been operational, the Corporation has put in place a mechanism that would allow for the creation of demand-driven large, for-profit skills training ventures linked to jobs and employability, with the onus on the skills provider to ensure the employment of at least 70 per cent of the people they trained.

From big corporates such as Centum (Bharti Group), TVS, Future or NIIT to NGOs such as Pratham, or from education institutions like the Centurion Group of Orissa to social entrepreneurs, there has been a growing interest among organizations to align with the NSDC to start sustainable skill development ventures.

Corporate groups have increasingly started seeing merit in setting up skilling ventures of their own or supporting the skills mission by hiring skilled workers at all levels. Enquiries on how organizations could associate with the NSDC have increased substantially, which is turn, has resulted in more proposals being submitted and approved for funding by the NSDC Board.

Importantly, again the proposals for skill development have encompassed diverse spheres and different geographies.

By seeing its role as that a social venture capital-cum venture debit/ development bank and putting its own skin in the game through patient capital, flexible financial terms and also a transparent and time-bound project approval, funding and monitoring frame work, the NSDC has enabled its partners to make a business out of skills.

Each skill development project proposal (including capex-heavy models generally oriented towards engineering/manufacturing skills) submitted to the NSDC is thoroughly evaluated by external financial and legal due diligence partners and then approved by an independent Project Approval Committee before the final sanction for funding is given by the NSDC Board. Each project is evaluated on the basis of several parameters that include assessing the market demand for trained manpower of the targeted sector, comprehensive evaluation of the course curriculum with more focus on practical training to meet industry standards and a study of the model followed for sourcing of trainers and collaborations with various corporates for placements to ensure that the business model is a holistic one.

NSDC has established a comprehensive monitoring framework which is out-come focused and monitors projects at different stages of their life cycle. With such a system in place, information on various aspects, such as, for example, the sector-wise training done, social excellence and financial excellence of the various models and states where the model is successful and where it needs to be reworked, can easily be gathered. Such an analysis by the NSDC also comes in handy for a partner to develop models for the dynamic and ever-evolving skill development industry.

Till June 2012, the NSDC Board had committed funds to 65 projects, of which 52 are pure-play training proposals and 13 are Sector Skill Council initiatives. Till June 2012, NSDC partners had trained over 210,000 people across India and ensured jobs for over 160,000 of the young boys and girls who enrolled at their institutions to pursue skill development courses.

Till June 2012, NSDC partners had set up 3,788 physical and mobile training centres and established a presence in 365 districts nationwide. NSDC partners have rolled out 403 courses that meet the skill development requirements of both the organized and unorganized sectors. Significantly, the capacity creation by NSDC partners has taken place not just in the bigger cities and towns but also in remote and far-flung areas and small towns and villages.

Special skills training initiatives of the NSDC have been helping youth in restive parts of north and north-east India to join the mainstream and participate in and contribute to the process of economic growth. NSDC has been able to get some of India's biggest corporate groups interested in the private sector-led skills training programme for graduates and post-graduates in northern India.

NSDC is ensuring a transformation in the skills arena with a new class of social entrepreneurs emerging in India.

In the last few years, the skill development landscale in India has evolved tremendously. Various changes have happened at the centre and state levels, involving the private sector at various stages

However, the biggest challenge in the skills space still lies in reaching the masses with quality training while keeping costs low at the same time Scaling up of sustainable models still poses a big challenge since each state and sector has different challenges to deal with.

The overwhelming response from the private sector to partner the NSDC is a clear proof of the fact that with a proper model in place, the public-private partnership approach can succeed.

All said and done, through, there is no getting away from the fact that skill development still has to establish deep roots in India.

Skill Development is a national priority and needs a coordinated approach by combining separate areas of government action on workforce participation, social inclusion and innovation so that policies on skills can connect with the wider economic employment and social strategies.

19

Sector Skill Councils

As per National skill Development Policy 2015, National Skill Development Corporation (NSDC) would constitute SSCs with following functions:

- Identification of skill development needs including preparing a catalogue of types of skills, range and depth of skills.
- Development of sector skill development plan and maintain skill inventory.
- Determining skills/competency standards and qualifications and getting them notified as per the NSQF.
- Standardization of affiliation, accreditation, examination and certification process in accordance with the NSQF as determined by the NSDA.
- Participation in the setting up of Affiliation, accreditation, and certification norms for their respective sectors.
- Plan and facilitate the execution of Training of Trainers along with NSDC and States.
- Promotion of academics of excellence.
- Will lay special emphasis on the needs of the ST/ST, differently abled and minority populations in the fields of employment and employability.
- SSCs shall ensure that the persons trained are assured of finding employment at decent wages.
- Conduct skill based assessment and certification which is based on QP and NOS developed for respective sectors.

Sector Skill Council are set up as autonomous industry-led bodies for steering skill development and training. They create Occupational

Standards, develop competency framework, conduct Train the Trainer Programs, affiliate Vocational Training Institutes, conduct skill gap studies in their sector leading to a Labor Market Information System and Occupational Standards developed by them

Achievements

Since their approval by the NSDC Board, SSCs have

- Over 350 corporate and Government leaders are represented in the Governing Councils of the SSCs.
- SSCs have a full-fledged professional team with domain and functional expertise.
- 22 Operational SSCs have created 943 Qualification Packs with 2,908 unique Occupational Standards. These have been validated by over 1000 companies.
- 19 Sector Skill Councils Have assessed and certified more than 15 lakhs such trainees.
- SSCs have affiliated 719 Training Organization having 17,250 centers, 29 Assessment Agencies with 2808 Assessor are affiliated to the Sector Skill Councils.
- SSCs have tie-ups for in –house training of organization employees – like Retail, Rubber, Plumbing; Automotive etc. over 500 companies have indicated that they will prefer SSC certificate holders.
- Through NSDC, SSCs work with multiple agencies including Central Ministries, State Governments, Educational Bodies and Institutions, and others operating in the skills development space.
- SSCs also provide through leadership in sector-specific growth objectives of State Government thus enabling an ecosystem for investments and job creation for certified and skilled manpower.
- SSCs also address challenges faced by specific groups including persons with disabilities, local governance institutions like Panchayats, rural entrepreneurs, etc.

Sector Skill Councils

No.	Sector	Name of the SSC
1	Automotive	Automotive Skills Development Council
2	Security	Security Sector Skill Development Council
3	Retail	Retailers Association's Skill Council of India
4	IT-ITeS	IT-ITeS Sector Skill Council
5	Media	Media & Entertainment Skill Council
6	Rubber	Rubber Skill Development Council
7	Healthcare	Healthcare Sector Skill Council
8	Gems & Jewellery	Gems & Jewellery Skill Council of India
9	Electronics & Hardware	Electronics Sector Skill Council of India
10	Agriculture	Agriculture Skill Council of India
11	Telecom	Telecom Sector Skill Council of India
12	BFSI	Banking, Financial Services & Insurance (BFSI) Sector Skill Council of India
13	Leather	Leather Sector Skill Council
14	Food Processing	Food Industry Capacity & Skill Initiative
15	Logistics	Logistics Skill Council
16	Plumbing	Indian Plumbing Skill Council
17	Capital Goods	Capital Goods Skill Council
18	Construction	Construction Skill Development Council of India
19	Life Sciences	Life Sciences Sector Skill Development Council

(Continued)

(Continued)

No.	*Sector*	*Name of the SSC*
20	Aviation & AeroSpace	Aviation & AeroSpace Sector Skill Council
21	Iron & Steel	Indian Iron & Steel Sector Skill Council
22	Power	Power Sector Skill Council
23	Mining	Skill Council for Mining Sector
24	Textiles & Handlooms	Textiles Sector Skill Council
25	Apparels	Apparel, Madeups & Home Furnishing Sector Skill Council
26	Beauty & Wellness	Beauty & Wellness Sector Skill Council
27	Handicrafts	Handicrafts & carpets Sector Skill Council
28	Tourism & Hospitality	Tourism & Hospitality Skill Council
29	Infrastructure Equipment	Infrastructure Equipment Skill Council
30	Sports	Sports, Physical Education, Fitness and Leisure Sector Skill Council
31	Oil & Gas	Hydro Carbon Sector Skill Council
32	Chemical & PetroChemical	Chemical & PetroChemical Sector Skill Council
33	Coating & Painting	Paints and Coatings Skill Council
34	Green Jobs	Skill Council for Green Jobs
35	PwD	Skill Council for PwD
36	Domestic Workers	Domestic Workers Sector Skill Council
37	Furniture & Fittings	Furniture & Fittings Skill Council
38	Instrumentation	Instrumentation, Automation, Surveillance & Communication Sector Skill Council
39	Strategic Manufacturing	Strategic Manufacturing Sector Skill Council
40	Management	Management & Entrepreneurship and Professional Skill Council

20

Issues in Skill Development and Training

The priorities/challenges in Skill Development and Training can be grouped under the following; (i) quality and relevance, (ii) quantity, (iii) expansion of outreach and equity, and (iv) systematic reforms.

Quality Issues

Quality Issues: Quality and relevance of skill development are key to India's global competitiveness as well as improving and individual's access to decent employment. To increase the relevance with future labour market including promotion of self-employment, soft skills and entrepreneurship skills need to be made integral parts of skill development.

Mismatch in demand and supply: The second major issue in skill development is mismatch between the demand and supply of skills. The problem has arisen due to supply driven skill delivery system. Presently the labour market is facing a strange situation, where on the one hand, an employer does not get manpower with requisite skills and on the other; millions of job seekers do not get employment. Such a mismatch compromises potential economic development. This requires:

- Establishing a mechanism for providing access to information on skill inventory and skill map on real time basis.
- National Qualification Framework to ensure both vertical and horizontal mobility and clarity of career choices, options and acceptability of the qualifications.

- Building skills training as a mainstream and inclusive programme to be promoted by creating a formal arrangement among the three key stakeholders in the delivery process: Government, Industry and Skills providers.
- Focus on International Collaborations to have better understanding of the fast changing skills demands and provide skills solutions that transfer the models practices and reverse the best practices from India to world.

Industry participation and Setting up of Sector Skills Council: In order to make the skill development system relevant and driven by labour market signals, it is necessary to increase participation of industries through Sector Skill Councils. Functions of SSCs could include inter alia, identification of skill gaps, preparation of Skill Development Plans and establishment of well-structured sector specific Labour Market Information System to assist planning and delivery of training.

Quantity Issues

Limited capacity: The first major roadblock in expanding the outreach is our limited capacity to absorb all those joining the Labour Market. As per Twelfth Plan projections about 25 million new entrants would join the labour force in the next 5 years.

Shortage of Trainers: Training of trainers is a key component of the skill development. There is an acute storage of trainers not only in the existing trades but also in the proposed new trades. There is an argent need for improving the quality and size of trainer resource. Skill up-gradation of trainers, there quality assurance, and improvement of their status in society are important to improve the quality of training. It is the pedagogical expertise of the trainer which ensures that the learner get a wholesome experience, understands the standards and is fully equipped to apply the concepts learnt during his employment. The Training of Trainers hence becomes a major challenge. As per the NSDC report on Education sector there is an incremental requirement 86, 64,000 teachers and trainers between 2008 and 2022.

Expansion of Outreach and Equity

India's large geographical territory comprising of 6, 38,365 villages, 4,378 towns in 35 states/UTs and 640 districts with difficult terrain and varying social-economic condition make the implementation of standardized skill-training a huge challenge. 11 most populous States like Bihar, with a population greater than that of Germany). Jharkand, Uttar Pradesh, Chattisgharh comprising 80 per cent of India's population with little access to skills training need to be taken up on priority. About 90 per cent of the 15-59 year olds have had no vocational training. Of the 10 per cent who received vocational training, only 2 per cent received formal vocational training. Therefore, access to skill programmes is a major challenge. Moreover, many emerging fields are coming up for which vocational training is needed (such as Nano Technology. Green Initiatives and so on) so as to maintain relevance with recent changes. The need is to implement the customized training depending on the geographical differences, capacities of the local people and requirement of the industry. Providing opportunities of skill development to all sections of society irrespective of any economic, social, regional, gender, spatial and sectoral divide is necessary to achieve faster and inclusive growth and for development of a just and equitable society.

Systemic Reforms

National Skills Qualification Framework: Currently there is no system in place which provides a framework to whole skill development and training sphere. There are no standards set in many areas creating problems for all the stakeholders. It is therefore needed to implement and run NSQF effectively.

Labour Market Information System: Dynamic and relevant inputs are important for taking informed decisions. Presently, there is no system where the stakeholders of employment and training, namely Government. Industry, Job seekers, private vocational training setups and so on can stream relevant information on a common ICT platform and benefit there from.

In order to address the issues relating to quantity and quality improvement; expansion of outreach and equity and systemic and institutional reforms a time bound action plan in terms of well-defined implementation and operational strategies with focus on the delivery of the skill is the need of the hour. The key strategies that need to be followed are given below:

Implementation Strategies

- Expanding outreach to bridge all divides
- Improving quality through better infrastructure, new machines and technology and trainers;

- Defining standards for outcome driven training programme and regular monitoring;
- Introducing flexibility by adopting global standards and dynamic process to suit the requirement of both national and international users;
- Developing strong partnerships between all stake holders, encouraging private partners through incentives;
- Creating enabling environment and monitoring the training programme to achieve outcomes.

Operational Strategies

- Replicability and scalability; strengthening existing centers;
- Linking training with outcomes;
- Affordability across economic levels;
- Stress on inclusivity and technology and innovation;
- Flexibility in course content; qualification standards; quality trainers; and
- Focus on delivery.

21

Skill Development Challenges

Alongside the daunting challenge of skilling millions of youth entering workforce each month, India also faces a huge challenge of evolving a skill development system that can equip the workforce adequately to meet the requirements of the industry. The workforce needs to be trained across four levels, from the high end specialized skills for 'White Collar' jobs to the low-level skills of the 'Rust Collar' jobs. Moreover, these skills have to be adequately linked to the available job opportunities.

Several factors have inhibited the skill development eco-system in India to scale up to the desired levels. The skill development system in India is plagued with multiple issues related to awareness, perception, cost, quality and scale.

FICCI pointed out the following five issues: (1) Inadequate scale, limited capacitylimited capacity" limited capacity", (2) Awareness, mandate and perception, (3) Cost concerns, (4) Quality concerns, (5) Mobility concerns.

Inadequate Scale, Limited Capacity

The existing infrastructure, both physical and human, is grossly inadequate considering the projected demand for skilled labour. While there is a need to create additional capacity in existing institutes, at the same time there is a need to create an adequate infrastructure even in small towns and villages.

In terms of faculty, too, the training infrastructure is inadequate. For instance, corresponding to the current seating capacity of about 1.7 million trainees at it is, there is a need of almost 85,000 trainers (considering 20:1 student/faculty ratio). As against this, the seating capacity for various trainers' programme of DGET is just 4.438, which is far from adequate to meet the requirement.

Awareness, Mindset and Perception Issues

Skill development in India is way below the requirements due to lack of awareness on the type of courses as well as information on the ensuring career prospects. More importantly, there is limited acceptance of skill development courses as a visible alternative to formal education. Skilling is often viewed as the last resort meant for those who have not been able to progress in the formal academic system. This is partly to do with the lack of integration between the two options and also due to raising aspirations for white collar jobs which necessitate higher qualifications. Moreover, skill development is often associated with blue collar jobs, which is largely perceived to be of low dignity and provides low wages/salaries.

The perceived 'stigma' associated with skill development has resulted in low enrolments in vocational education courses. The aspirational mismatch that exists is India can be gauged from the example of the construction sector, which has a huge requirement of workforce with low level skills. For instance, the construction sector in Punjab faces a shortage of workforces with locally, and depends on the migrant workforce from Uttar Pradesh, Bihar and Jharkhand.

Cost Concerns

Skill development initiatives in India continue to be largely dependent upon the government funds or public-private ventures. Owing to high capital requirements and low return on investments, skill development is often looked at as a non-scalable model and remains underinvested. Additionally, a fee-based model also faces challenges as prospective students are often unwilling or unable to pay high fees for training. Even the bank's willingness to lend for skill development activities is low as educational loans are perceived as high risk products due to uncertainly with respect to future employment.

Quality Concerns

There is a serious mismatch between the industry's requirements and the skills imparted in educational and training institutes, especially for the mid-level skills requiring some expertise on handling of machinery. To tackle this problem, considerable improvement of the quality of training is needed.

The issue relates to the quality of infrastructure, trainers, as well as curricula and pedagogy. In terms of infrastructure, the institutes, often lack appropriate machinery to give students hands-on training. Even the course curricula often are outdated, redundant and non-standardised. Additionally, the lack of industry-faculty interaction on course curricula leads to irrelevant training modules.

The availability of good quality trainers is also a key concern. The quality of trainers is affected due to limited efforts towards re-training and skill improvement of trainers. There is a lack of focus on development of trainers with a clear career path which can make this an aspirational career choice and can ensure regular adequate supply of good-quality trainers in every sector.

While there is a need to constantly upgrade the training infrastructure and pedagory, it is very expensive. This restricts the pace of modernization and upgradation. Likewise, the process of standardization is challenging in India. a significant portion of total employment falls under the unorganized segment, where it is extremely difficult to sensitise the employers on the importance of occupational standards, job role and qualification packs.

Mobility Concerns

In India, educational qualification is generally preferred over vocational training as former is associated with better employment opportunities, in terms of pay as well as quality of work. Additionally, there is limited mobility between formal education and vocational training in India due to lack of equivalent recognition for the latter; a student enrolled in vocational training often cannot migrate to institutes of higher education due to eligible restrictions.

However, under the on-going National Skills Qualification Framework (NSQF), attempts are being made to address the mobility issue by recognition of prior learning and establishing a credit system for skills, knowledge and experience gained by an individual either formally or informally. NSQF is expected to enable multiple-entry and exit between vocational education, skills training, generally education, technical education and job markets.

The Way Forward

The Indian Government has laid a special focus on expanding and improving the skill education and training in the country. The New Policy on Skill Development and entrepreneurship contains several initiatives which, if implemented earnestly, will go a long way in minimizing the demand-supply gap and challenges related to skill mismatch with industry requirements.

With increased thrust on manufacturing under the 'Make in India' programme, the need for revisiting and improving India's skill development mechanism becomes all the more critical. It has been globally recognized that an efficient vocational education and training plays a critical role in the industrial development and manufacturing success, as in the case of economies like Germany and China. The study of skill development model of three countries done in this report highlights some best practices that can be utilized in India's skill development eco-system.

Integration of skill development with formal education system, mobilization of students for skill development by removing misapprehensions and perceptions about vocational trades, investing in creation of new training capacities for students as well as teachers, utilization of idle public infrastructure to provide skill training in remote corners of the country, encouraging industry to actively participate in training through provision of apprenticeship as well as through direct involvement in curriculum design and teachers training, adopting innovative skill development delivery mechanisms are the much-needed steps to meet the skill related challenges today.

There is a scope of international collaboration and assistance in India's skill development initiatives at almost all levels, including for creating awareness and capacities, setting standards, improving quality, as well as providing placement opportunities.

FICCI suggested the following specific measures that can be taken by various stakeholders including the government, industry bodies, corporate, educational institutes as well as foreign investors and international agencies.

The Way Forward for Skill Development

Addressing Issues: What is required?	*Proposals under National Skills Policy and recent Govt. initiatives*	*Policy suggestions: What (more) needs to be done and how?*
1. Creating awareness and mobilization		
Spreading awareness on the need for skilling is critical. Awareness is required for all stakeholders including students, parents, industry, teachers as well as trainers.	- National campaign to be launched to create awareness and promote skilling. The delivery mechanisms will include dedicated television channel, community radio as well as social media.	- Awareness on need for skilling should be taken up in mission mode and activated at the local level, including states, districts and villages.
- A perception change with respect to skilling is required in society. Parents and students need to look beyond traditionally preferred jobs and traditional delivery mechanisms of education and training.	- A National Portal for skilling will be created, which will also include a Labour Market Information System (LMIS). This system will provide information on sectors, modules, training opportunities, etc. to enable students to make students to make informed choices. It will also aggregate data on all persons mobilized and seeking skill development training.	- Different communication mechanisms should be adopted for each level. For example, SSDMs can organize advertisement campaigns in vernacular language through electronic as well as print medium.
- Industry, especially SMEs, need to be informed about the benefits of engaging skilled vis-à-vis unskilled people. They also need to be informed about various institutes/centers that supply skilled students for particular trade.	- Skill India Logo to be used to promote value of skilled workforce and encourage certified skilling. Industry will be encouraged to move towards employing certified skilled people and to rationalize compensation by awarding skill premium for increased productivity due to higher skills.	- School can be engaged effectively for counseling students at early stages (e.g. class 5) about vocational education, apprenticeship and associated career paths.

(Continued)

(Continued)

Addressing Issues: What is required?	*Proposals under National Skills Policy and recent Govt. initiatives*	*Policy suggestions: What (more) needs to be done and how?*
- Industry should recognize the training/skill development offered as per national occupational standards and offer skilled workers premium in pay.	- Prime Minister's Skill Development Fellow Scheme to be introduced wherein selected candidates will work with State and District administration to spread awareness related to Skill development.	- School staff and teachers to be sensitized about vocational training and apprenticeships as potential career paths for students.
	- IT and Mobile technology to be utilized to develop platforms for connecting demand and supply of skilled workers.	- Encourage students to opt for vocational stream in schools by providing incentives like stipend for rural students for boarding and lodging, lowering or making tuition fee free for students from economically weaker sections (Such incentives are provided in China due to which enrolment in vocational education is very high there)
	- Special mechanisms in delivery of training such as mobile training units, flexible afternoon batches, training based on local area needs, etc. will be introduced to ensure participation and mobilization of women.	- Counselling sessions should be organized for parents, highlighting some national and international case studies.
		- Introduce financial incentives for employers for employing apprentices, retaining apprentices as permanent employees and for employing the disadvantaged. Such financial incentives may be linked to performance.

2. Creating capacities/infrastructure		
- Significant new capacities need to be created for training for different trades across the country. Hence, novel ideas would have to be developed to utilize the existing infrastructure with government for skill development purpose.	- Government plans to incentivize use of existing infrastructure for adding training capacity; the infrastructure that can be made available includes 1.55 million schools, 25,000 colleges, 3,500 polytechnics, 1,50,000 post offices, 100,000 kiosks, and 65000 km of railway network with 8000 stations.	- The Rajasthan SLDC has been implementing an innovative model of movable training institutions (mobile vans/buses) for some of its remote geographical pockets. A similar model can be used across India to provide training at village levels and thereby encourage rural population, especially women, to take up training for specific skills and earn a living.
- To address the issue of migration, training infrastructure needs to be created close to the catchment areas including sourcing cluster.	- New ITIs in PPP mode to be set up as Multi Skilling Institutes (MSIs).	- Use of information technology through e-education and training should be widely adopted to create virtual capacities.
	- Massive Open Online Courses (MOOC) and virtual classrooms to be developed for delivery of vocational education.	
3. Integration, Mobility and Transition		
- Vocational education needs to be integrated with general e3ducation in schools and colleges.	- National Universities for Skill Development will be institutionalized which will include a network of state level institutions affiliated to it.	- NSQF is a step in the right direction and it has to be ensured that all institutions make a collective effort in aligning their qualifications as per the set standards.

(Continued)

(Continued)

Addressing Issues: What is required?	*Proposals under National Skills Policy and recent Govt. initiatives*	*Policy suggestions: What (more) needs to be done and how?*
- Additionally, the course curriculum should be made practical, in line with industry's requirements, and constantly upgraded through feedback from the industry.	- Vocational training to be integrated into formal education by introducing vocational education for four years from class 9, in the least 25 per cent of school. Skill courses will be independent subjects that will also carry qualifying marks for admission to higher levels. Pilot projects have already been running in a few states (e.g. Haryana, Karnataka).	
- There has to be a seamless facilitation from secondary to higher education if a student chooses to study vocational courses. This would also encourage more students to opt for vocational training as the fear of not being abled to pursue higher education in the future will not be there. The Australian VET system allows easy movement in and out of vocational training which offers flexibility to students.	- Special focus will be laid on youth who do not wish to continue with school or higher education. Special programmes will be initiated for providing skill training to those who have eight years or more of schooling. NSQF as a means to integrate and provide multiple pathways between general and vocational education will help school drop-outs make choices about vocational courses.	

- The National Skills Qualification Framework (NSQF) includes reorganization of prior learning and establishing a credit system for skills, knowledge, and experience gained by an individual either formally or informally. NSQF is expected to enable multiple entry and exit between vocational education, skill training, general education, technical education and job markets.
- All formal and vocational education including skills training will have to be aligned with the NSQF by December 2018.
- Multi Skilling Institutes (MSIs) will be affiliated to Skill Universities, and provide a bridge into general higher education through diplomas/certificates based on a credit framework aligned to the appropriate NSQF level.
- Polytechnics will be converted into community colleges, which will provide NSQF-aligned vocational courses along with Bachelor's degrees in vocational studies.
- At least 25 per cent of all existing higher education institutions would offer additional career oriented courses with specialized skills at an appropriate level of NSQF.

(Continued)

(Continued)

Addressing Issues: What is required?	*Proposals under National Skills Policy and recent Govt. initiatives*	*Policy suggestions: What (more) needs to be done and how?*
	- Kaushal Vardhan Kendras (KVKs) to be set up at village level to mobilized and impart skills to school drop-outs, adolescent girls, housewives and rural youth to enable them to secure a sustainable livelihood.	
4. Greater Industry linkage		
- Dual systems like that in Germany integrate work-based and school-based learning and impart more practical skills. The system of apprenticeship needs to be encouraged and could be made mandatory for specific vocational courses.	- Training curricula will be developed in consultation with industry representatives, experts and academia.	- The Higher Education policy needs to be in line with present and projected employment opportunities, and hence there should be a focus on revising the curriculum and offering relevant new courses.
- Industry exposure to student will help in acquiring relevant skills and improve the prospects of placements.	- Industry houses including MSMEs will be incentivized to institutionalize paid apprenticeship.	- Incentives can be devised to encourage firms (including MSMEs) to undertake regular apprenticeship programmes. This may include provision of tax incentives, grants for part funding, etc.

- Industry linkage is also important for faculty training to keep them abreast of latest changes.	- Training providers should tie-up with industry in relevant trades for improving placement opportunities for students. Government support to training providers will be linked to the placement performance and tie-ups with industry.	
5. Financing mechanism		
- Skill development requires at least partial state funding. The problem of under-investment by different stakeholders is often addressed by creating infrastructure and providing financial assistance for skill development. A combination of public and private funding is demonstrated to yield the best results.	- Government to support creation of training infrastructure in public and private domain through equity, grant and loan support.	- Innovative funding mechanisms need to be evolved to encourage greater enrolments in skills-development initiatives.
- Since it is not feasible for the state to undertake the entire cost of skill development skill development, incentive mechanisms that induce private players and students to invest much be instituted. The funding framework of China can serve as a good example.	- It is proposed that the industry should earmark at least 2 per cent of its payroll bill (including for contract labour) for skill development initiatives in their respective sector.	- Government may consider setting up a training fund to facilitate financing of poor students for pursuing vocational training.

(Continued)

(Continued)

Addressing Issues: What is required?	*Proposals under National Skills Policy and recent Govt. initiatives*	*Policy suggestions: What (more) needs to be done and how?*
	- Government to promote grant of scholarships, rewards and skill vouchers for funding of training costs for those with an inability to pay the training fees. Skill Vouchers can be redeemed by the training providers based on a performance linked payment schedule subject to successful completion of training.	- Students are willing to take huge loans of their higher education but not so skilling,. Innovative ideas need to be evolved to encourage students take out loans for skill training too. First of all, skill courses need to be made more attractive by ensuring placements and attaching a premium to the pay for higher skill capabilities. Cost of funds for willing students can be lowered by introducing interest subvention scheme for skill related loans, providing tax exemptions towards repayment of such loans, etc.
6. Quality improvement - The standardization process to improve the quality of vocational education and training is already the process but need s to be expedited. National Standards for each occupation should have national as well as international recognition.	- All the National Occupational Standards (NOS) and Qualification Packs (QPs) developed by Sector Skill Councils for various trades will be examined and reviewed by the National Skills Qualification Committee (NSQC) before being 'National Standards'. Thereafter, all vocational training in the country will have to align these 'National Standards'.	- More ITIs need to be upgraded with respect to course content, equipment and technology. ITIs, adoption by private enterprises should be encouraged.

- The ITIs need to be upgraded in terms of equipment, course content, as well as faculty.	- NSQF will be aligned to globally recognized standards. Transnational standards will be created for specific trades having potential opportunity to international workforce mobility. - National Universities for Skill Development and Entrepreneurship to be promoted as an institute of excellence for skill development and for training of trainers. - Industry representatives will be encouraged to become guest faculty at Multi-Skilling Institutes. Industry professional will also be empanelled as adjunct faculty in relevant areas for teaching during off-hours. - Standards certification for trainers will be institutionalized.

22

Chief Ministers on Skill Development

A Sub-Group of Chief Ministers on Skill Development was constituted on 24th March, 2015 following the first Governing Council meeting of NITI Aayog to address the issues related to scale, speed, standards and sustainability of the ambitious goals set for the Skill Development Mission.

The Sub-Group felt that the major challenges to be addressed in this journey are making skill aspirational among youth; addressing mobility between education and work; improving access and outreach; providing quality trainers; monitoring outcomes and making available adequate financial resources. Since States are the major players there is need for an integrated delivery framework at the State level to ensure convergence of programs by strengthening the State Skill Development Missions. However, it was felt tat there should be total convergence at the Central Government level also and all Central Ministries should comply with the common norms and standards formulated by Ministry of Skill Development and Entrepreneurship. The States of the North East as well as less industrially advanced states have, on their part, urged that there should be Central Government support as well to help them in taking forward the skilling initiatives in their States.

Sub Group's Recommendations

1) Integrated Delivery Framework for Achieving Convergence

- The State Skill Development Missions (SSDMs) should evolve into a coordinating body to harmonize the skilling efforts across line departments/private agencies/voluntary organizations etc. The common norms announced at the central level may be adopted by the SSDMs so as to have state-specific guidelines for skill developments programmes.

- For decentralized implementation and to ensure effective coordination and monitoring of skill developments initiatives a three-tier structure at state, district and block level for SSDMs proposed. Pattern of DRDA to coordinate skill efforts at district level can be adopted for effective coordination and interaction with local self-government, civil society, training providers, industry and other stakeholders.
- Determination of sectoral priorities at State level based on an independent assessment of the needs of each sector and the formulation of appropriate policies to enhance the qualitative and quantitative skill availability for the sector based on conduct of regular skill surveys.
- SSDMs should have the overarching power to pool across the resources and to utilize according to priority. The inter-linkage of the SSDMs with the industry, training providers, Sector Skill Councils, NSDA should be maintained at the policy formulation and implementation level.
- Sector Skill Council to assist the State Skill Development Missions to align training program with NSQF.

2) Achieving Scale and Relevance through PPP

- Industry to be incentivized to set up training institutions in PPP mode in industry clusters to facilitate availability of trained manpower for big and MSME units and to adopt existing governments ITIs and Polytechnics.
- Local industry to be involved for curriculum development, training modules, provision of equipments, training of trainers, opening skill developments centres and taking apprentices.
- Industry can also enter into flexi MOU based on sector, trade or institutions and offer work benches for practical training.
- Industry can help in developing a database of instructors as also resilient system for selection of training providers.
- The States Government can incentivize the public sector or the private industries operating either within the State or in neighboring regions to involve in the skill development efforts

of these States through their SSDMs in less industrialized as well as difficult terrain.

- Skill Development programmes and skill training providers should get an extension of service tax exemption for the next 5 years.
- Income tax exemption to category-A training providers (as per the definition of Ministry of Rural Development) for a period of 5 years need to be considered.
- Skill training in manufacturing sector should be incentivized in all skill development programmes to achieve the broader objective of "Make in India programme".

3) Reaching the Unreached and the Disadvantaged

- The possibility of introducing legislation on Right of Youth to Skill Development to make it mandatory on the part of the State to impart skill training to every eligible youth may be explored.
- Vocational education may be introduced from the middle level onwards with SSDM having the responsibility to explore the marketability potential of traditional skill sets of the State. This would motivate the children to take up training in traditional skills especially in States that excel in handicrafts, wood art and handlooms. Further the international models viz German, Chinese and Singapore may be studied for replication in India.
- Flexibility to states to introduce local and traditional skills meeting local needs to be provided under various central government administered skill programs and attract local youth for training.
- Opening of Incubation Centres, Counseling Centres and Tracking Centres at the village level.
- The provision of safe transportation, female instructors, child care facilities, market and finance to encourage women participation. Also making available dormitory/hostel facilities in district and block headquarters for students from remote corners.
- Using ICT, mobile vans, to make available training facilities in villages and hilly areas.
- Monetary and non-monetary incentives should be part of the policy for training providers and potential employers to engage with differently-abled persons.

4) *Improving the Quality*

- SSMs could play a facilitating role to address the shortage of instructors/trainers especially in imparting practical training by identifying Government/private/self-employed entrepreneurs operating establishments/units in the skills in demand in the State and bring them on the panel where students after attaining the basic skills can be sent for practical training.

5) *Making Skills Aspirational by involving Local Bodies/NGOs*

- The Railways and other para-military forces can play a more proactive role in advocacy and skill development, instead of just focusing on recruitment rallies. The personnel of these agencies could be used for skill training or these agencies could lend institutional support in imparting training in hilly, inaccessible and difficult terrains.
- The awareness among the targeted population on the benefits of skill training can be generated through audio/visual media as well as through street plays and by involving the PRIs/ULBs and Civil Society.
- Local Bodies to be used for skill mapping and creating a data base of youth at local level.

6) *Focus on Outcome*

- Union Government initiatives in strengthening the National Career Guidance Centre at the district and block level, integrating with the Labour Market Information System should be facilitated by the SSDMs. This would facilitate to track the youth receiving skill training and moving to placement either as self-employed or wage-employed.
- LMIS/National Career Service Centers could be the medium where the success stories that are documented can be shared so that provides a medium for the youth to explore the possibilities of its up-scaling/replication.

7) *Making Available Adequate Resources*

- To enhance the scale of skill development resources is of utmost priority. Half of the 2 percent CSR could be used exclusively for skill development initiatives. Further it was also agreed to by the Sub-Group that out of the cess collected under the Building and other Construction Works Cess Act, 1996 the Cess Fund which is presently in surplus should be available for imparting skill training to all underprivileged youth irrespective of whether or not they are wards of construction works.

- Public Training Institutions to be made revenue generating.
- Use of MPLAD/MLA funds for creating infrastructure for skill development could be explored.
- Funds generated under education cess could also be used for introducing vocational education from secondary school onwards.
- MOSDE should make a budget provision for all States to set up Skill Universities or convert one of the existing Universities as a Skill University under PPP mode. This funding could be made available through NSDF/NSDC.

23

Training and Skills Development in the East Asian Newly Industrialised Countries

In this narrative briefly the skill development system is examined in Korea, Malaysia Singapore, Taiwan and China and Common characteristic and differences are established and lessons are drawn.

Common Features

When the government mandates that a certain amount of training must be provided, there is usually an expansion in the amount of training being offered. However, it is not always clear whether this is useful in increasing skills; neither is the effect on their quality clear. When the government confines itself to the regulatory side, that is, in monitoring, evaluation and certification of training programs and in dissemination of information, the results (both in terms of quantity and quality) are more positive. Training policies can have equitable or inequitable effects. Often larger firms and more educated workers benefit more than smaller firms and the less qualified workers. In general, employers prefer in-house training (and training has higher returns) to training being offered by outside contractors. Reforms of training have been undertaken regularly as conditions change. The NICs amend or abandon interventions frequently, often responding to signalling from changing economic conditions.

Paradoxically, the speedy industrialization of recent years has resulted in a greater increase in training in commercial, language, information technology, management and related courses rather than in industrial skills.

This has been accompanied by more autonomy of institutions over time and greater participation of employers. Increasingly institutions develop their own admission policy and are responsible for the selection of their own staff. Cost-recovery has been increasing and systems are becoming more flexible and demand-driven. Private sector specialist providers of training tend to concentrate in areas where costs of provision are relatively low and demand is high. This is often the case in urban areas and it is not surprising that in Singapore this form of provision is most widespread.

There are some cross-country similarities in training across some industries. Training is more important in transport, machinery, in metal extraction, communications and the utilities but to a lesser degree in the electronics industry. Training is unusual in the construction industry, probably because of the high labor turnover rate in this sector. Other industries in which training is relatively uncommon include food and textiles, both of which use relatively unskilled and predominantly female labor.

Often vocational schooling at secondary level contains a high general education component. In general, the opening of trade has increased the provision of/demand for a more general type education. The education system in Singapore has undergone a series of reforms in order to keep provision in line with the current state of economic development. The rapid shift of the Taiwanese economy from agricultural to industrial has imposed demands on the system, which has had to adapt rapidly to the changing economic environment.

Labor market outcomes of vocational school graduates are in general characterized by lower earnings and less promising employment prospects than academic graduates (even after controlling for factors that affect the two groups). This is partly due to the prevalence of public training centers that impart less effective training though they often have higher costs and higher staff/student ratios.

Differences

There are some notable differences with respect to both the general policy framework within which decisions are made and also to specific training provisions.

Training institutions and the production sector are coordinated centrally in some countries (such as Korea and Singapore) but this is not so evident in others (such as training in Taiwan, China and production in Malaysia).

Foreign direct investment (FDI) and the role of large firms in general Singapore than in the other countries. Largefirms employing sophisticated technology are particularly active providers of in-service training, and this often applies to the case of multinational enterprises.

While in many countries the public sector is dominant in the provision of vocational education and training, several of the NICs, notably Korea and Singapore provide exceptions. Many training programs are provided by private sector organizations even though they may be funded (in part or whole) by government.

Some countries operate a levy/grant system or a 'train or be taxed' policy. Firms in Korea are effectively taxed, but they can avoid this expenditure by training their workers. In light of this observation, the preference of many firms in Korea to incur tax losses is no more surprising – and represents no more a failure of the system – than would an accumulation of surpluses in Singapore's Skills Development Fund.

In some industries there is substantial cross-country variation in training. Training is deemed to be very important in the financial services and the tourism sectors in Singapore but not in Korea or Taiwan, China. This might reflect differences in the level of development, and in the size and openness of the economies in question.

Vocational secondary education has been pursued in some countries but not in others. Taiwan, China has pursued secondary vocational education vigorously, albeit with a high general academic content. Korea is on a similar pattern. On the other hand, Malaysia's poly-ethnic composition has resulted in an educational policy that attempts to foster national unity and moral development through academic rather than vocational education.

Lessons

There is no universal prescription for training interventions. Much depends on country-specific characteristics such as simple or sophisticated production, the availability of information, size of country, the nature of labor, product and credit markets, and the kind of industrial policy the government has chosen to pursue (centralized or laissez-faire). The socially optimal provision of in-service training, therefore, depends on the developmental stage of the country.

The first lesson is that skills development systems should delay specialization as much as possible, and specialized occupation-specific aspects of training should take place in-service. Too early specialization can divert significant resources from more productive uses to expensive, but often ineffective, training. The track record of vocational training within the formal education sector has been disappointing. This has led to a general move away from vocational secondary schools though this trend is bucked in some countries (such as Taiwan, China) where vocational secondary education appears to offer high rates of return (comparable to those obtained in the academic schools). However, vocational education in Taiwan, China has a high content of academic courses. The low social rates of return to vocational education and the high rates observed in the case of in-service training suggest that the fundamental question in skills development is not whether to vocationalize schools but at what stage in the education process. A country that has a 40 per cent enrollment ratio in primary education or 3 per cent in secondary education is unlikely to realize positive social returns from vocationalization. However, a country with universal secondary education can start introducing vocational/technical courses in the curriculum.

The second lesson is that administrative measures that increase the private provision or finance of training should not act as a tax and be simple in design. The experience with levy/grant or 'train or be taxed' schemes is mixed. Taiwan, China abandoned the scheme. Korea is constantly amending it. In Singapore disbursements for training are lower than the revenue collected for this purpose. The financial incentives schemes in Malaysia are unduly complicated and have a low take-up rate. Political considerations may also be important. The high incidence of non-training in Korea is partly because firms successfully put pressure on the Government to keep the tax rate down. Overall, levy-grant schemes require competent tax mechanisms that are not usually well developed in many developing countries and have elements of dead-weight.

The third lesson is to allow public and private providers of training to operate with autonomy that would enable them to supply skills in demand in an effective way. Internally, this means that training providers should have freedom to select their own students, recruit staff and choose courses and, externally, their coordination should be undertaken by independent bodies.

The fourth lesson is that active participation of employers enhances the performance of training. In-service training contracted freely at the workplace has low costs and high returns. The heterogeneity of in-service vocational training schemes and measurement problems have restricted the number of cases where returns to training are. When available, rates of returns of in service training are particularly high enterprise training has produced social rates of return of 20 per cent in Malaysia, and in-plant training for welders in Korean shipbuilding had a rate of 28 per cent, higher than in non-firm training institutions.

The fifth lesson is that a regulatory function of the government and continuous monitoring and analysis of the labor market are useful instruments in ensuring that adequate skills are created in a timely manner and at minimum costs.

24

Engagement with Other Countries

The Ministry of Skill Development and Entrepreneurship has engaged actively with several countries with the purpose of technology transfer in skill training, training of trainers, setting up of model and centres of excellence. In addition, active collaboration is being sought in the area of creation of international mobility through mapping of job roles and development of transnational standards. Overall, the strategy for International framework focuses around implementing and adapting the best practices in skill development of respective countries systems in India. The following MoUs have been signed by the MSDE/ or its organizations.

MoUs Signed by MSDE or its Organiasations

Country	*Agency/Dept/ Organization*	*Signed By*	*MoU*	*Expected Outcomes/Deliverables*
United Kingdom	UK India Education & Research Initiative	MSDE	Mar, 2015	1) Institutional capacity building of UK and Indian officials and institutions handling skills development. 2) Sharing of technical expertise, building linkages and identification of gap in the ereas of skill development, curriculum development and reform, benchmarking of assessment, accreditation models, and certification and training methods. 3) Sharing of best practices in approved areas including policies on skills development, credit framework designs, occupational standards and apprenticeship models. 4) Joint activities such as validation of National Occupational Standards and other initiatives on Sector Skill Council engagement through the National Skill Development Corporation (NSDC) and UK Commission for Employment and Skills (UKCES) 5) Joint activities on teacher training and use of ICT, MOOCs and other digital initiatives. 6) Underpinning collaborative research or study to focus as decided on priority areas 7) Joint training on entrepreneurship development in approved areas.
	Association of Colleges UK	NSDC	Jan, 2014	Member colleges of AOC and NSDC Training Partners to collaborate in support in building training capacity, functional skill assessments, international benchmarking in certifications.

	Department for Business, Innovation and skills on Behalf of the Government and the Devolved administrations of the United Kingdom of Great Britain and Northern Ireland	DGT (then under MoLE)	Nov, 2013	1) Institutional capacity building of UK and Indian official and institutes handling skill development and employment services 2) Sharing of technical expertise, building linkages and identification of gaps in the areas of skill development and employment service, improvement in curriculum, benchmarking of assessment, certification and training methods. 3) Supporting development of employment services in India on the lines of National Careers Service, UK.
	UKCES (UK Commission on Employment and Skills	NSDC	Mar, 2011	UKIERI funding support Indian and UK counterparts to jointly bid for projects primarily for execution in India related to Skill Development and/or SSC collaboration. The project aimed to support NSDC in establishing a network of Sector Skills Councils and their capacity building in India through a series of workshops. Aspects included promotion, contracting, funding, performance management, impact assessment, Standards and Qualifications, Qualification frameworks and supporting the incubation of two SSCs, in Agriculture and Media Sectors.
Germany	IMOVE (International marketing of Vocational under BiBB)	NSDC	May, 2011	Knowledge transfer and fosterning of private sector initiatives and collaboration in VET between Indian and German stakeholders (SSCs/Chambers, training providers, research institutions, corporations and other public and private entities)

(Continued)

(Continued)

Country	*Agency/Dept/ Organization*	*Signed By*	*MoU*	*Expected Outcomes/Deliverables*
	Federal Ministry for Education and Research of Federal Republic of Germany	DGT (then under MoLE)	May, 2011	1) Creating Public Private Partnerships (PPP) on pattern of German dual system. 2) German assistance in upgrading Vocational Training Institutions in India. 3) Training of Trainers (ToTs). 4) Sharing and development of competency standards 5) Mutual recognition of qualifications. 6) Development of content and instructional material. 7) Strengthening Research & Development. 8) Assessing Labour Market demand and converting it into training modules.
	TAFE SA and Heraud	NSDC	Jan, 2015	A Global Standards Multi Skill Development Centre to be setup by TAFE SA in partnership with Heraud Training & Education in Delhi NCR.
Australia	TAFE directors Australia	NSDC	Nov, 2014	1) Joint cooperation in baseline curriculum support for targeted vocational education training 2) Reciprocal staff exchange and study tours to develop professional capability 3) Advanced teacher training programs for technical trainers and teachers 4) Joint symposium with senior NSDC and TDA Australia TAFE

	Australia Council for Private Education & Training (ACPET)	NSDC	Nov, 2014	Promote strategic partnerships between ACPET members, NSDC and NSDC Training partners
	Department of Industry, Australia and now shifted to Department of Education	NSDC	Sept, 2014	1) Developing transnational standards to strengthen skills mobility by making NOS transnational in 4 sectors (Auto, Healthcare, Telecom & IT) across 8 job roles. 1) Capability building of TVET trainers and assessors in India
USA	US Community Colleges		Apr, 2015	3 loan proposal from: • Houston Community Colleges, Texas • Lone Star Community College, Texas* • Alamo Community College, Texas *MoU Underway – Work has started with colleges Objective: To set up Academies of Excellence in India mainly in Capacity Building of the type and quality matching International Standards. Each entity is committing to create minimum 50,000 qualified skill Trainers & assessors in a period of 10 yrs. Additionally, the objectives include developing expertise in areas of curriculum development, teaching and learning resources development, occupational standards, testing and certification etc.

(Continued)

(Continued)

Country	*Agency/Dept/ Organization*	*Signed By*	*MoU*	*Expected Outcomes/Deliverables*
	US-India Business council (USIBC)	NSDC	Nov, 2014	To work with US companies to ensure that in a span of 3 years, they support 10 training centres that are expected to scale to reach a capacity of around 10,000 persons per year. Over a 10 years period these centres should be able to train 1,000,000 people. The specified sectors are Life Sciences, Healthcare, Tourism, Hospitality, Automotive, Electronics, Heavy Equipment Manufacturing, FMCG, Aviation, BFSI, IT/ITES, Agriculture, Defense and Infrastructure.
Canada	Associate of Canadian Community Colleges	NSDC	Feb, 2014	The following 3 categories of MoUs have been signed a) Community Colleges: 1. Seneca College – Non – Technical Aviation 2. Canadore – Technical Aviation 3. Fleming – Water 4. College of New Caledonai – Hydrocarbons 5. Algonquin – Construction 6. Southern Alberta Institute of Technology – Hydrocarbons 7. Blow Valley and Camosun College – Sports 8. Camosun College – Healthcare 9. Durham College – Agriculture and Automotive 10. Fanshawe – Apparel & Textile b) CICan (College & Institutes Canada – erstwhile Association of Community Colleges of Canada) c) SSCs: Eco-Canada to assist Green Jobs SSC; ICTC-CTIC to assist IT, Telecom & Electronics SSCs

				Objectives: Community colleges – 10loan proposals to set up Academies of Excellence in India of the type and quality matching International standards. Each entity is committing to create min 50,000 qualified skill Trainers & Assessors in a period of 10 yrs. Canadian SSCs – to jointly work with Indian SSCs on developing NOS & transnational standards to enhance the mobility of labour. The objectives also include curriculum development, teaching & learning resources development, testing & certification etc.
Singapore	Ministry of Education Singapore	DGT	Jul, 2012	1) Capacity Development in Vocational Education & Skill Development (VE&SD). 2) Institute of Technical Education may help in the capability development of India's VE and SD officials and staff. 3) Advisory Services: ITE may provide advisory services to enhance planning, management and delivery of VE and SD in India, Including the setting up of vocational training institutes/centres or schools.
European Union	European commission	NSDA	Jun, 2014	1. Enhanced capacity of the beneficiary Institutes to apply and adopt a European best practice perspective as and where relevant in work relating to skills development. 2. Substantial progress made in the development and maintenance of the national qualification framework for India, including the National Occupational coding 3. Labour market information systems and analysis practices enhance at the national level and the state level on a pilot basis.

Continued)

(Continued)

Country	*Agency/Dept/ Organization*	*Signed By*	*MoU*	*Expected Outcomes/Deliverables*
France	CNCP (Commission Nationale de la Certification Professionnelle CNCP)	NSDA	Jan, 2015	Work out methods of cooperation in the area of qualifications register between India and France
Iran	TVTO (Technical and Vocational Training Organisation)	NSDC	Jul, 2014	Starting of NOS & QP with training providers to support IT based training systems.
China	MHRSS	MSDE	May,2015	The main areas of cooperation in the MoU are establishment of sub-centres near the industrial park in Vododara, advisory and knowledge sharing, development and designing of courses and curriculum, skill standards, qualification framework and competency standards, participation by business entities and industries from China and India, development of business models for skill development in PPP mode.

25

International Context: Best Practices in Skill Development

Some of the international experiences in skill development can be suitably adopted in the Indian context. Skill development ecosystem in Germany, Australia, China, United Kingdom and Singapore are briefly described here. These countries have succeeded in developing an efficient skill system

1. Germany

Germany largely follows a dual-system of vocational education and training (VET). The system is called "dual" because training, under this system, is conducted in two places of learning: in the enterprise and in the vocational school. The company provides practical training, and vocational school supplements this on-the-job-learning with theoretical instruction and basic economical background.

The dual system is especially well-developed in Germany, integrating work-based and school-based learning to prepare apprentices for a successful transition to full-time employment. The dual-system is the largest provider of education and training at the upper secondary level. Around 75 percent of young people enrolled in VET take part in the dual system of vocational training.

The dual system has been a major factor in Germany's economic success and inventiveness over the past six decades. Many countries have looked at Germany's dual education system when reforming their own VET/Skills education system.

The Dual Vocational Education and Training (VET) Mode

Dual VET programmes are currently offered in 349 trades and can take between two and three-and-a-half years. Germany's dual system of vocational education and training (VET) is a very simple and cost-efficient model.

- The practical training (approx. 70 percent of training duration) takes place in companies. This training is based on a compulsory curriculum, which is adapted to conditions of the training company and is monitored and controlled by the respective chambers, who also arrange for the interim and final examinations (comparable to sectoral skill councils). This in-house training is guided and imparted by certified corporate trainers. The 'apprentices' undergoing training sign a vocational training contract with the company and are paid a training salary by them.
- The theoretical part of the training (approx. 20 percent of training duration) is taught in vocational schools, run by the State governments.

Salient Features of Germany's Skill Development Eco-system

Mobility: Dual-system like the Germany one integrate work-based and school-based learning and thus impart more practical skills. This offers greater flexibility to students in terms of the choice of courses and career options.

Flexibility: Flexibility is a key characteristic of successful skill-development initiatives. VET in Germany imparts practical training and thus ensures that the curriculum and training is abreast with changes in technology or other changes in the industry.

Industry Linkage: Companies engaged in VET are also constantly involved in the process of upgrading and modernization of curricula. Industries play a crucial role in identifying future requirement of skills and update training regulations to meet that demand. Under the guidance of the Federal Institute for Vocational Training and Education, experts from companies, industrial chambers and trade unions develop the training regulation for the apprenticeship program.

Funding/Financing Mechanism: The VET system as a whole is well-resourced, combining public and private funding. Enterprises bear the cost of in-company training and pay the trainee remuneration as regulated by collective agreement.

Under the dual VET, the responsibility for funding vocational schools lies with the "Lander" i.e. the provincial/state government (for teacher salaries) and local authorities (equipment, infrastructure).

Incentives/Benefits for Stakeholders

The system proves advantageous for all stakeholders.

- The government does not need to equip the vocational schools with expensive machinery necessary for practical training suited to industrial needs. It has to only guarantee theoretical training in vocational schools with well-trained teachers. This saves the cost of investing into equipment and machinery.
- Companies train students in real working processes and with well-equipped state-of-the-art machinery. Since companies already have expensive equipment for their operational requirements, there is no separate cost incurred for arranging expensive equipment only for training. All costs incurred by companies engaged in VET are considered an investment.
- While the students are trained on-the-job, they also become more productive. Additionally, if the companies can retain apprentices as employees, they benefit from lower recruitment costs, reduced costs of on-the-job training and benefit of having skilled workers suited to company requirements. Yet there is no regulation that binds the company to take over students once they complete their VET.

Standards/Quality

The VET system of Germany is known for imparting quality training of high standards. Training regulations in the country require adherence to a uniform national standard which corresponds to the requirements in the relevant occupation. Only those training enterprises can carry out training exercises whose training personnel are appropriately qualified to impart the skills as required by the training regulation. Under the dual system, companies also have to train and employ certified corporate trainers within the company.

Social Integration (for Disadvantageous)

To provide education to those students who do not manage the transition from lower secondary education to the VET system directly through normal routes, a 'transition system' was developed. It strives to help young people to achieve apprenticeship readiness, to enable them to obtain some form of school-leaving qualification and to act as a bridging measure until they are able to enter regular vocational training. Under the 'transition system', students who do not have school-leaving certificates are enrolled in one or two-year programmes in full-time VET schools, which do not lead to a VET diploma but offer the opportunity to obtain the intermediate secondary school-leaving-certificate. After obtaining the required education, students can enter into vocational training through Dual Apprenticeship Training.

2. Australia

Australia's Vocational Education and Training is an integral part of the overall education system in the country designed to deliver workplace specific skills. The system has been very successful, reflected in high participation rate of adults in vocational training.

Australia's VET system is characterized by competency based training, which is concerned with capability based outcomes rather than duration of course/training. Additionally, the system allows a person to gain formal qualification regardless of how or where the training was delivered.

VET Structure

VET is a sophisticated system governed by interconnected government and independent bodies functioning within a National Skills Framework of Qualifications defined by Industry Training Packages and the Australian Quality Training Framework (AQTF).

VET is delivered by registered training organizations (RTOs). Training providers who want to provide accredited courses have to apply to become an RTO and can be either government or private providers. Government registered training organization include Technical and Further Education (TAFE) institutions, secondary schools and colleges, universities, agriculture and technical colleges and community organization providers.

Apprenticeship under VET

In Australia, apprenticeships and traineeships are available to everyone as no formal entry qualification is required. Apprenticeships are available at different certificate levels and for more than 500 occupations in most sectors of business and industry.

Apprenticeship can be delivered through following alternative ways:

- Australian school-based apprenticeships, which allow students from year 10 to combine completing school and starting an Australian apprenticeship;
- Full-time Australian apprenticeship wherein apprentice spends the whole week with on-the-job training (about 80 percent of time) in the company and off-the job training with a chosen training provider;
- Part-time Australian apprenticeships which are often used by small and medium sized enterprises. A minimum number of hours of on-the-job and off-the-job training per week are provided to the apprentice (e.g. 15 hours per week).

Under the apprenticeship system, a legal contract between an employer and an apprentice is necessary, which determines the training wags and conditions. Apprenticeship wages differ according to the level of qualification, training year, industry and the type of apprenticeship (school-based, part-time or full-time). In addition, the employer has to determine a training plan with details about on-the-job training, which has to be endorsed by the chosen training provider.

Salient Features of Australia's Skill Development Eco-system

Mobility: The Australian VET system allows easy movement in and out of vocational training. This offers greater flexibility to students in terms of the choice of courses and career options. Students enrolled in the VET programme can also opt to enter into tertiary education provided they have the necessary qualifications required to do so. The transition between VET programmes and higher education is possible due to 'articulation' agreements which allow credit transfers between these two parts of the education system.

Accredited courses lead to different AQF qualification: Certification I and II (which take between 1-2 years); Certificates III and IV (2-4 years); VET Diplomas (2years); and VET Advanced Diplomas (2-3 years). After completing III, IV, VET Diploma and VET Advanced Diploma, student can obtain Graduate Diploma and Graduate Certificates by undertaking education and training for 6 months and 12 months respectively. These two qualifications and VET Diplomas/ Advance Diplomas can be accredited towards higher education degrees.

Flexibility: Australia's VET system is flexible as it allows learners to achieve completed formal qualifications, single certified modules or courses without formal qualification. By allowing a selective approach to training, it does not force participants to complete qualifications.

Additionally, the system allows recognition of prior learning Registered Training Organizations (RTOs) are required to recognize AQF qualifications and statements of attainment which have been issued by other RTOs. Also, if one already has competencies achieved from prior learning, these can be assessed and certified directly, reducing the training period and facilitating the switch between qualifications.

Due to its flexibility, Australia's VET is suited for nearly all types of people-those who enter the workforce for the first time, those who wish to re-enter the workforce after a period of absence or those who want to update or upgrade their skills. Furthermore, the VET system provides a wide range of programmes which address specific learner groups (such as culturally appropriate training for indigenous Australians; courses for people with disabilities; English courses for immigrants, etc.)

Industry Linkages: Another efficient characteristic of Australia's VET system is the strong influence of industrial bodies on VET policies and priorities, which enables matching of skills training to the industry requirements.

The National Industry Skills Council is the nodal organization which gives advice on training matter including training needs, future training priorities and workforce planning. In order to guarantee strong industry leadership in the VET system, 11 Industry Skills Councils exist which collect information about industry training needs from employers, unions and professional industry associations. They develop training packages and give advice training matters

Funding/Financing Mechanism: On the whole, the VET system in Australia is funded by the federal and regional governments, employers and individuals. All three parties involved in intermediate VET have costs and benefits of intermediate training. Companies which provide on-job training are also eligible for Australian Government funding.

Standards/Quality

The AQF is a comprehensive and nationally consistent framework which regulates post compulsory education. The AQTF is a national set of standards which help to ensure there are nationally consistent, high-quality training and assessment services in the VET system. The national sets of standards give assurance to the industry that particular quality standards are met when training takes place under this framework.

Social Integration (for Disadvantageous)

A transition system known as the Intermediate VET system contributes to social integration and allows attaining VET qualifications for participating in the labour market. The system provides opportunities for catching up on missed training and providing lifelong learning for an ageing workforce. It is applicable for 'second-chance students' who previously failed at primary or secondary education. Besides, the intermediate VET system also addresses the inclusion of disadvantaged of groups such as people with disabilities, and people coming from weak socio-economic background.

3. China

The Chinese Technical Vocational Education and Training (TVET) is a comprehensive system which is systematically planned to meet the needs of vocational education and training at different levels. To meet the challenges of China's industrialization drive, the government has repeatedly taken initiatives to reform China's TVET system. The Vocational Education Law of 1996 provides the legal framework for the implementation/functioning of the vocational education and training system in the country.

Through its vocational education law, China ensured cooperation between vocational institutes/schools and society, enterprises and villages, and became market-oriented through methods such as learning and practice, learning while working, emphasizing on practical and vocational competence skills.

China's skill development model has been highly successful and developed at a rapid pace. In China, 59 percent of those entering the workforce are skilled, of which 39 percent are vocationally trained. China's skill development model has enabled transforming of its high schools into skill-training centres, and successfully promoted internships for the vocationally-trained. Around one third of young people in China today enter vocational upper secondary schools.

Structure

The system of vocational education consists of (a) education vocation schools and (b) vocational training. The formal school based vocational education is under the Ministry of Education (MOE) and has a slight emphasis on theory based training; while vocational training is under Ministry of Human Resources and Social Security (MOHRSS) and focuses on post-school, pre-employment, and on-the-job practical training, as well as training and re-training for those out-of-school or out of work.

The education law of China mandates nine years of compulsory education including three years of vocational training. Vocational education and training in the school system is provided at three levels: junior secondary, senior secondary and tertiary while VET outside the schooling system is provided through adult learning and enterprise training.

Salient Features of China's Skill Development Eco-system

Industry Linkage: In China, school-education as well as vocational training offer practical training to the students/trainees. Industry participation in vocational education and training is ensured through the 1996 Vocational Education Law. As per the policy directive, each student should spend one year on workplace training during their upper secondary programme. Industry participation is thus a built-in-characteristic of the entire TVET system.

The enterprises also participate in curriculum design, teacher training, provision of training equipment in the schools, and placing students for internship etc.

Industry is also given various incentives to encourage industry participation in vocational training, for instance allotment of land subsidized prices, and preferential treatement in case of award of government projects.

Decentralized and Locally Driven Skill Development Initiatives: Most of the skill development programmes in China are highly decentralized, run by the local government and village collectives. The local governments are given a say in deciding a part of the curriculum in accordance with the local needs. The curricula of senior secondary vocational schools are designed such that, one-third includes general academic skills defined nationally by the Ministry of Education, another third are nationally defined content associated with the particular occupation, and the remaining third are determine locally at the school level with the help local enterprises. For instance, in Chongqing, the shares of primary, secondary and tertiary sectors are 8, 55 and 37 percent respectively. Accordingly, the focus of trades in curriculum for the respective sectors is 7, 52 and 41 percent respectively.

Funding/Financing Mechanism: The 1996 Vocation Education Law requires that 20 percent of the annual education budget should be allocated to vocational education and training. Due to a fiscally decentralized economy, education in China is subject of the local government. As much as 89 percent of the funds for education are raised by the local governments.

Additionally, all enterprises are_required to utilize 1.5 percent of their payroll towards in-service training. If they fail to do so, equivalent amount should be contributed to the government for adult training.

Mobility: The link between secondary and tertiary vocational education and various training programmes has been planned such that vocational education is not perceived as a 'dead-end'. Under the VET system, horizontal and vertical mobility of VET graduates is allowed because of the national level College Entrance Examination. Consequently, a large proportion of graduates from secondary vocational schools continue with higher education.

Standards/Quality

The government has made huge investments in providing quality infrastructure for VET, which includes buildings and teacher tools for programmes. China has strong arrangements to ensure that teachers in vocational schools remain abreast of the requirements of modern industry. Teacher in vocational schools are required to spend one month in the industry each year, or two months every two years.

Social Integration (for Disadvantageous)

The government provides subsidies to groups of workers who have trouble finding employment to attend training programmes. Targeted populations include registered unemployed people, rural migrants, and rural labourers

- To overcome the financial burden and to ensure that the poor students continues in VET schools, a national scheme was introduced to offer a subsidy of 1500yuan per year per student, for their first two years at secondary vocational schools to cover their fees.
- Since 2009, an initiative has been taken to make senior secondary vocational schools free of cost for all students. As per law, students with financing difficulties or disability are to be provided with tuition fee waivers for vocational education and training.

Additionally, Chinese education policy is based on life-long learning and thus gives due recognition to adult literacy and training. For rural workers engaged in agriculture, government provides applied technical training in agriculture which includes green certification training and entrepreneurship training. In 2011, there were 103,420 technical training schools for adult farmers with around 35 million registered participants. Of these, the majority of schools were run by education departments and collectives of the villages. The strong extinction system, coupled with training for rural agricultural workers not only improves agricultural production, but also provides an incentive for the rural workers to stay back rather than migrate to cities restricting rural and urban migration of untrained workers.

4. United Kingdom

The National Vocational Qualification (NVQs) were created in response for the felt need for qualifications to be made flexibility but rigorous and nationally recognized. NVQs are also part of 'Modern Apprenticeship' which are funded through work-based learning. The funding varies between occupational sector and by age group. The national framework covers general secondary and tertiary education, VET, work-based learning and prior learning. Accreditation of Prior Experiential Learning (APEL) describes the process of giving formal recognition to learning that derives from personal experiences often gained in employment or voluntary work situation.

At the industry level, Sector Skills Councils (SSCs) have been licensed and social partners are also engaged. SSCs are tasked with drawing up occupational standards for their sector that will feed into the national reform of qualifications. The Government expects each SSC to draw up a Sector Skills Agreement, in which employers and unions identify skills and productivity needs in their sector and the necessary to meet those needs.

5. Singapore

The National Skills Recognition System (NSRS) is Singapore's national framework for establishing work performance standards, identifying job competencies and certifying skills acquisition. It in implemented by the Standards, Productivity and Innovation Board with the support of the Ministry of Manpower and the Ministry of Trade and Industry. This has helped the industry train skills-standards consultants and assessors, as well as to develop. On Job Training (OJT) blueprint for the skills-standards established. To assess the workers, assessment centres were set up. Workers can be certified at centralized assessment centres, workplace or a combination of both.

Supporting the NSRS implementation framework are promotional activities and financial incentives for the industries. NSRS is promoted at four levels, i.e. national, industry, company and workforce, in collaboration with employer groups, industry associations, economic agencies and unions.

Appendix I

Skill Development and Training Programmes of Central Government

Sl. No.	*Ministry/ Department*	*Schemes/Programmes/Institutions having provision for Vocational Education and Training programmes*	*Target Group*	*Duration of Training (long-term/Short-term)*
1	M/o Agriculture (i) Department of Agriculture research & Education	Training in Agriculture Extension (21 training centres), Training in use of Agricultural Implements & Machinery, Soil Conservation Training centre, LFQC&TI, NPPTI Cooperative Education and Training.	Person engaged in agricultural institutions and support services, members of cooperatives and farmers. Under KVK, 550/589 districts are covered.	Short terms courses
	(ii) Department of Animal Husbandry, Dairying & Fisheries	Under the University stream various under-graduate and Ph.D. courses are offered (DARE).	Students with Qualifications as usual under University stream of education.	U.G courses – 4 years (ex-cepts for veterinary courses i.e. of 5 years), P.G courses -2 years and Ph.D. as usual.
		There is one Central Agricultural University, thirty-one State Agricultural Universities (SAUs) and four National Institutions of Indian Council of Agricultural Research having the status of Deemed to be University.	Students with Qualifications as usual.	As usual.
		ICAR also arranges need based training programmes in any of State Agriculture University or ICAR Institutes in new and emerging areas.	Individual scientists or groups of scientists.	One week to three months (or longer duration, as fixed).
		CIFNET – Regular courses (2) and special training courses (14)	10th Standard students	6-18 months

		CIFNET – Refreshers courses (4)	Lecturers/in service	4 weeks
		CIFNET – other Organisations viz college including engineering and forign nationals (14)		3 days to 14 weeks
2	M/o Food Processing Industries	Grants were provided to NGOs for setting up of 326 Food Processing & Training Centres (FPTCs) during 1992-93 to 2000-01.	Person living in rural areas with	Short term
		Institutions like Central Food Technology Research Institute, Processing Research Centre, PHTC, Council of Entrepreneurial Development programme (EDP) are also running training courses.	Mainly persons in Food Processing Industry	SHORT-TERM
		Person power development in rural areas (FPICs scheme)	Open	SHORT-TERM
		Entrepreneurship Development Programme	Open	AICTE approved diploma/ degree courses duration as usual (Long -term)
		Programmes for development of human resources in food processing, testing, training, quality management etc.	Candidates aspiring to be managers, technicians/technologists and entrepreneurs	
3	M/o Healthy & Family Welfare	Basic training of multipurpose health worker (female & Male) • 478 ANM/MPW(F) training Centres • 28 HFWTC & 30 Basic MPWa (M) schools	Educations youth with minimum 10th pass	12 to 18 months

(Continued)

(Continued)

Sl. No.	*Ministry/ Department*	*Schemes/Programmes/Institutions having provision for Vocational Education and Training programmes*	*Target Group*	*Duration of Training (long-term/Short-term)*
		Promotional training of Female Health Assistant in 42 trainings centres. Training is also provided by Safdarjung Hospital, St. John Ambulance, NTCP, NPCB, NMHP, NACP, INC, CBHI, CLTRI, PWTRC, ECH etc	Person working in Health & Family welfare programme	Short term
4	M/o Heavy Industries & Public Enterprises	Counseling, Retraining and Redevelopment of Rationalized Workers of CPSEs (Formerly NRF)	Workers who opt for voluntary retirement, rendered surplus or retirement from CPSEs	Short term courses
5	M/o Human Resource Development	Vocationalisation of Secondary Education (6800 schools covered)	Student having passed 10th class	2 years
		Polytechnics (1244) + Institutions for diploma in pharmacy (415), hotel management (63), architecture (25)	10th pass	3 years diploma
		Community Polytecnic Scheme (675 CPs)	Disadvantaged groups of adults. Priority is given to adult neo-literates/semi-literates, SC and ST, women/girls, oppressed, migrants, slum/pavement dwellers and working children	Need Based (1-4 weeks)
		Jan Shikshan Sansthan		

		(157 Vocational Training Centres run by NGOs offering more than 250 courses)	Engineering and physical sciences under- graduates/post graduates in the country, all teacher/faculties in science and engineering universities in India	(Designing course material – time bound project)
		Support For Disance Education & Web Based Learning (NPTEL)	School leavers with 5th, 7th, 8th and 10th pass	6 months to 2 years
		National Institute of Open Schooling Distance Vocational Education Programmes [Practical training through Accredited Vocational Institutes (AVIs)]	Student passing out of +2 Vocational stream	One year
		Apprenticeship Training for student of +2 Vocational stream	Recognized engineering colleges/ polytechnics and schools of architecture having related academic degree or diploma programme	Faculty development through short -term crash programmes and long-term programmes
		National Programmes on Earthquake Engineering Education (NPEEE)		
6	D/o Information Technology	DOEACC-'0' level	Student or working persons with 10+2 pass	Flexible duration for passing examination
		CEDTI	It conducts courses in the field of Electronics, Telecommunication IT, Process Control & Instrumentations	Short term courses

(Continued)

(Continued)

Sl. No.	*Ministry/ Department*	*Schemes/Programmes/Institutions having provision for Vocational Education and Training programmes*	*Target Group*	*Duration of Training (long-term/Short-term)*
7	M/o Labour (DGET)	Craftsmen Training Scheme (CTS) (5114 ITIs)	School leavers with 8th 10th and 12th pass	One to Three years
		Apprenticeship Training Scheme (ATS) (20,800 establishments)	School leavers with 8th 10th 12th pass or National Trade Certificate (from NCVT) Holder	6 months to 4 years
		Crafts Instructor Training Scheme (CITS) (6 Institutes)	Instructors of it is	1 year
		Advanced Vocational Training Scheme and HI- tech Training Scheme (65 Centres)	Industrial Workers/Technicians	Short term Courses
			Supervisory from Industry	Long and short term
		Supervisory Training (2 institutes)	Women (School leavers, Instructors and others)	Long and short term
		Women Training Institutes (11 institutes)	Training Executives and Principals	Short Term
		Central Staff Training and Research Institute	School leavers with 8th, 10th and 12 pass	One to Three years
		Model Training Institutes and Model Industrial Training Institutes		
8	M/o Rural Development	National Institute of Rural Development (NIRD) Conducts about 150 programmes	Practicing Manager in rural development	Short term Courses

		Swarnjayanti Gram Swarozgar Yojana (SGSY)	Focus is on the vulnerable groups among the rural poor. SC/STs should account for a minimum of 50 per cent women for 20 per cent and disabled for 3 per cent of the total swarozgaris during a year.	Need based short term
9	M/o MSME	Entrepreneurship Development Programme, Skill Development Programme (SDP), Management Development Programme • It has 72 institutes/bodies • SSSI – 30 • Br. SSSI – 28 • Rtc – 4 • Tool rooms – 8	• Workers • Educated unemployed youth • Entrepreneurs	Both short term and long term
10	Khadi and Village Industries corporation	51 Training Centres run 35 types of programmes	Unemployed rural youths In- job Artisans/Supervisors working in KVI instts, Prospective Entrepreneurs, Benificieries of different Govt. Schemes desirous of undertaking KVI activities.	2 months to 12 months

(Continued)

(Continued)

Sl. No.	Ministry/ Department	Schemes/Programmes/Institutions having provision for Vocational Education and Training programmes	Target Group	Duration of Training (long-term/Short-term)
11	M/o Social Justice & Empowerment	National Institute in Mentally Handicapped, National Institute for the Orthopedically Handicapped, Institute for Physically Handicapped National Institute for the Hearing Handicapped, National Handicapped Finance and development Corporation, National Scheme of Liberation and Rehabilitation of Scavengers and their Dependents, National Scheduled Casts and Scheduled Tribes Finance and Development Corporation, Rehabilitation Council of India	Disadvantaged and marginalized sections of the society viz, SC, Minorities, B.C, Persons with disabilities, Aged Persons, Street children and victims of Drug Abuse etc	Short term training upto six months durations Orientation programmes upto one weekdurations
12	M/o Textile	Decentralized Training Programme, 24 Weavers' Service Centres Cooperative Training 13 Power loom Centres, Indian Jute Industries Research Association, Central Wool Development Board, Central Silk Board, Training Centres for Handicrafts, North – eastern Handicrafts and Handlooms Development Corporation	Skill upgradation of Workers in textile industry	Mainly short term (15 days to 3 months) Some courses under Handicrafts are of 1 year duration.
13	D/o Tourism	15 Food Craft Institutes under State Government	10th Pass	6 months – 1 years
14	M/o Tribal Affairs	Vocational Training Centres (VTC) in Tribal Areas (100 per cent central assistance is given to State/UT/ NGO for setting up VTs	Unemployed Tribal youth (Each person is given training in two trades)	6 months in VTC and 6 Months with master craftsmen

15	M/o Urban Development & Poverty Alleviation	Urban Self Employment Programme under Swarna Jayanti Shahari Rozgar Yogjana (SJSRY)	Urban Unemployed or underemployed poor below poverty line	Short term (2-6 months) subject to minimum 300 hours
16	HUDCO & others in Construction Sector	640 Building Centres (HUDCO)	Person engaged in Construction Industry	Short term courses
		Company run schools (NBCC HCC, L&T, ECC etc) & association etc		Short term courses
		Construction Industry Development Council (CIDC) & others	Worker & Supervisor having Qualification of Vth to XIIth Standard	1 month to 6 months
17	D/o Women & Child Development	Support to Training and Employment Programme for Women (STEP)	To provide updated skills and new knowledge to poor and assetless women traditional sectors	Short term courses
		Swalamban (previously NORAD	To train poor women mostly in non-traditional trades	
		Training in Home scale preservation of fruits and vegetables, (by Community Food and Nutrition Extention Units (CFNEUs)	House wives and Adolescent girls with a view to promote preservation and consumption of fruits and vegetables which provide much needed micronutrients, as well as to provide necessary skills which could be useful for income generation purpose.	Two weeks

(Continued)

(Continued)

Sl. No.	*Ministry/ Department*	*Schemes/Programmes/Institutions having provision for Vocational Education and Training programmes*	*Target Group*	*Duration of Training (long-term/Short-term)*
		Central Social Welfare Board (programmes are organized by voluntary organizations)	To train and equip adolescent girl To train women in marketable trades and also to upgrade their skills for getting remunerative employment opportunities s to improve home based and vocational skills	
		Women Empowerment Programme in collaboration with IGNOU (Training programme on "Empowering women through SHG")	To organize women into effective Self Help Groups	
		Kishori Shakti Yojana	To train and equip adolescent girls to improve home based and vocational skills	
		Other programmes like UDISHA, Training of Anganwadi Workers, NIPCCB, Rastriya Mahila Kosh etc.		Minimum 60 days

Appendix 2
Key Skill Development Schemes for Various Target Groups

Sl. No.	*Name of Scheme*	*Particulars/Objectives of the scheme*	*Duration of the Training Program (hours/days/ months*	*Any specific group scheme callers to*
1	Horticulture Mission for North East and Himalayan States (HMNEH)	HMNEH is being implemented for overall development of Horticulture in NE and Himalayan states. The mission addresses entire spectrum of horticulture from production to consumption through backward and forward linkages.	3 months-1 year (Farners-2 to 5 years)	Entrepreneurs, Gardeners, Farmers, Supervisors, Field Staff
2	Support to Artisans scheme. Sub-scheme of Integrated Leather Development Programme.	For providing employment opportunity & to fill the demand of operators in the footwear sector & improving the quality.	Short duration training programs (2 week to 1 month)	Artisans in rural clusters
3	Capacity Building and Technical Assistance (CBTA) scheme	Provide funding for skill development, enhancing of employability and competencies and promotion of self-employment and entrepreneurship amongst youth.	Varies (6 months- 1 year)	Youth from the North East Region, Special focus on girls, women, disabled persons and youth from BPL background and from remote and backward districts or unreached areas,

(Continued)

(Continued)

Sl. No.	*Name of Scheme*	*Particulars/Objectives of the scheme*	*Duration of the Training Program (hours/days/months*	*Any specific group scheme callers to*
4	Entrepreneurship Development Programme (EDP) by various govt. and pvt. Organizations, industries or NGOs	To enable trainees to establish commercially viable enterprises in food and agri-processing		SC/ST/Minority Community/Women At least 35 per cent
5	National Urban Livelihoods Mission (NULM)	Skill training to be provided for both Wage Employment (job placement) and Enterprise Development.	Minimum 3 Months (with 400 hrs of technical training & 30 hours soft skills training)	Urban poor
6	Jan Shikshan Sansthan (JSS) as a component of "Scheme of Support to Voluntary Agencies for Adult Education and Skill Development"	Jan Shikshan Sansthas (JSSs) are established to provide vocational training to non-literate, neo-literate, as well as school drop outs by identifying skills as would have a market in the region of their establishment.		Socio-economically backward and educationally disadvantaged groups in both Rural and Urban areas.

7	Vocationalisation of Secondary and Higher Secondary Education	To enhance the employability of youth through demand driven competency based modular vocational courses, to maintain their competitiveness through provisionbs of multi-entry multi-exit learning opportunities and vertical mobility/interchangeability in qualifications, and to reduce dropout rates.		Children from Class IX onwards i.e at the secondary stage.
8	Integrating Differently Abled persons in the mainstream of Technical and Vocational Education	To train the differently abled students in technical institutions by Ministry of Human Resource and Development (MHRD). The differently abled students were given both formal and non-formal training in the Polytechnics Colleges in India.	Few weeks to 6 Months (part time non formal)	Differently Abled
9	Pradhan Mantri Kaushal Vikas Yojana (PMKVY)	24 lakh Trainees to be offered monetary incentives and a government certification on successful completion of training and assessment, which will help them in securing a job for a better future.	Trainees with more than 3 months training	Target to aligned to the demand from the flagship programmes.
10	Craftsmen Training Scheme	Provide semi-skilled/skilled workers to industry by systematic training to school leavers; and Reduce unemployment among educated youth by equipped them with suitable skills for industrial employment. The scheme is implemented through government run ITIs and private ITCs. Under the scheme focus is on creating centres of excellence as also focus on difficult areas.	6 months – 3 years	School Leavers with 8th, 10th, and 12th pass, maximum of 50 per cent reservation depending on State SC/ST per cent, 25 per cent women, 3 per cent physically handicapped.

(Continued)

(Continued)

Sl. No.	*Name of Scheme*	*Particulars/Objectives of the scheme*	*Duration of the Training Program (hours/days/months*	*Any specific group scheme callers to*
11	Skill Development Initiative	Provide for skills up gradation/formation, vertical and horizontal mobility including recognition of prior learning for school drop-outs, unorganized sector workers etc,; and Facilitating multi entry and exit and allowing recognition of prior learning.	1 month to 1 year (Modular courses from 60 hours to 1000 hours)	Class 5th onwards as well as people with uncertified prior learning, at least 30 per cent women.
12	Apprenticeship Training Scheme	To utilize fully the facilities available in industry for imparting practical training with a view to meeting the requirements of skilled manpower for industry and thereby reducing mismatch Apprentice Protsahan Yojana (APY) would facilitate MSME also to engage the trainees	6 months to years	School leavers with 8th, 10th and 12th pass or NCVT holder. The Apprenticeship scheme to cover all categories of apprentices except the Graduate Technician and Technician
13	Women Training Institutes	Enhancing women training to increase women participation in the labour market. Training facilities	Short and long term	Girls 8th, 10th, 12th pass
14	Entrepreneurship Development Programs through MSME-	are being offered to women through 11 institutes spread across the country.	EDP- 2 Week, ESDP- 6 Week, MDP- 1 Week (FT) 2 Week (PT)	Workers, Educated unemployed youth, Entrepreneurs and their executives

15	Skill Development activities through Tool Rooms	Entrepreneurship Development Programs are being organized regularly to nurture the talent of youth by enlightening them on various aspects of industrial activity required for setting up MSEs.	Short term and long term programmes on High End Technology	Workers, Educated unemployed youth, Entrepreneurs and their executives
16	Multi-Disciplinary Training Centers (MTDC) and other training Centers of KVIC	Upgrade skills of prospective entrepreneurs, existing workforce and also develop skills of new workers and technicians of MSEs	Flexible, usually short term	Artisans, unemployed youth, supervisors etc.
17	Training by Coir Board on spinning of coir and production of value added products	To setup own units of cottage and small industry. The Multi-Disciplinary Training Centre of KVIC implements the programme.	Long term and short term	Rural women
18	Multi Sectoral Development Programme	Improving socio-economic conditions of minorities and providing basic amenities to them for improving the quality of life of the people and reducing imbalances in the identified minorities concentration areas	Varies	Minority youth
19	Seekho aur Kamao	To bring down unemployment rate of minorities; Conserve and update traditional skills of minorities and establish their linkages with the market and improve employability of existing workers, school dropouts etc and ensure their placement.	Modern Trades – Minimum 3 months	Minority youth

(Continued)

(Continued)

Sl. No.	*Name of Scheme*	*Particulars/Objectives of the scheme*	*Duration of the Training Program (hours/days/ months*	*Any specific group scheme callers to*
20	Pandit Deen Dayal Upadhyaya Grameen Kaushalya Yojana (earlier known as Aajeevika)	Training 10 lakh (1 million) rural youths for jobs in three years, that is, by 2017 and bench marking training against international standards. This would also address the needs of differently abled, marginalized youth and women in LWE districts	3 – 12 months	Rural poor youth (18 35 years) 33 per cent women, 50 per cent SC/ ST, 15 per cent minorities, 3 per cent differently abled.
21	Rural Self Employment and Training Scheme (RSETI)	Rural Self Employment Training Institutes (RSETIs) across the country as institutions to mitigate the unemployment and underemployment problem among youth in the country. this institute generate self employment in rural areas through training for capacity building and by facilitating in settlement in vocations.	1-6 weeks	Rural BPL youth
22	Hunar Se Rozgar Tak under Capacity Building for Service providers (CBSP) scheme	To create employable skills in the interested youth who are in the age group of 18 – 25 years and who are minimum 8th pass.	6-8 weeks	8th pass 18-28 years
23	Special Central Assistance to SC and Tribal Sub Plan	10 percent allocation of assistance is fixed for skill development of tribal youth	Varies	Scheduled Castes and Tribe youth

24	TRIFED-Skill development/upgradation and capacity building for Handicrafts/ Handlooms	TRIFED – a National level Cooperative Body under the Ministry of Tribal Affairs, Government of India, is engaged in the skill development/up-gradation and capacity building training of tribal handicraft artisans and tribal people along with marketing of their product. Skill Development & Capacity Building training of Minor Forest Produce gatherers and Training of Tribal Handicraft Artisans engaged in making Handlooms, Handicrafts, Tribal Paintings etc.	45 days (30 days training and rest 15 days in mass production)	Women and educated unemployed school drop out youths
25	Support to Training and Employment Programme for Women (STEP)	To provide skills that give employability to women. And to provide competencies and skills that enable women to become self- employed/entrepreneurs.	Less than 3weeks	Poor and asset less women in traditional sectors
26	Priyadarshini scheme to organize women into effective self help group	The 'women Empowerment and Livelihood Programme in Mild Gangetic Plains also called Priyadarshini Programme envisages holistic empowerment of 1,08,000 poor women and adolescent girls through formation of 7200 SGHs. The programme originally being implemented in six districts including four districts in Uttar Pradesh	Less than 3 weeks	Women

(Continued)

(Continued)

Sl. No.	*Name of Scheme*	*Particulars/Objectives of the scheme*	*Duration of the Training Program (hours/days/ months*	*Any specific group scheme callers to*
27	SABLA – Rajiv Gandhi Scheme for Empowerment of Adolescent Girls	The objective is to improve the nutritional and health status of adolescent girls in the age group of 11 – 18 years and empower them by providing education in life-skills, health and nutrition the Government of India introduced the SABLA in November, 2010. The Scheme also aims at equipping girls with information on family welfare health and hygiene existing public services etc, and to draw out-of-school girls into the formal or non-formal education systems	MES modules	Adolescent girls in the age group of 11 to 18 years
28	Skill UP-gradation Training Programme for Women in 200 Border/Tribal/ Backward Districts (SUTP)	The programme is aimed at enhancing the vocational skills of women in the border or tribal or backward districts and also at helping them to acquire self-employment. The programme enables women participation to supplement their income in existing occupation, improve productivity and learn new skills for which there is a good demand in the market.	Minimum duration of Skill Training Programmes should not exceed three months	Women from SC/ST, OBC Minority, Widow Economically Backward and Destitute/Homeless categories
29	Udaan	The Special Industry Initiative, known as "Udaan", targets the youth of J&K, specifically graduates and postgraduates, who are seeking global and local opportunities. It aims at providing corporate India with exposure to the rich talent pool available in the state.	Varies by sector	J&K youth

Appendix 3
Standardized Courses of Skill India Programme

Entrepreneurship cum Skill Development Programmes & Training of Trainers Programmes (EDPs)

- AC Refrigerator & Water Cooler Repair
- Agricultural Water Lifting Equipment – Maintenance & Repair
- Bakery Products
- Biotechnology
- Black smithy
- CAD/CAM
- Calibrations of instruments
- Carpentry
- Catering
- CNC Lathe Wire cut Milling
- Compressor Repair
- Computer Accounting with Tally
- Cosmetology and Beautician
- Cyber café
- Dairy based ESDP
- Designing and Manufacturing of Artificial Jewellery
- Die Fitter
- Draughtsmanship training
- DTP
- Electrical gadget repair
- Electronic Assembly
- Electroplating
- Fashion Designing
- Hosiery & Woollen Garments
- Essential Oil and Perfumery Products
- Food Processing
- Footwear Designing
- Forging and Casting
- Gaming with flash
- Glass Cutting & Polishing
- Heat Treatment
- Leather Products
- Lens Grinding
- Machining
- Microprocessor Application & Programming
- Microsoft Certified Software Engineering
- Mobile Repairing
- Motor & Transformer Rewinding
- Motor Winding & Pumpset Repair
- Mouldings & Pattern Making
- Multimedia
- Mushroom Cultivation
- PCB Design
- Photography and Photoshop
- PLC Programming
- Plumbing and Sanitary Fittings
- Retail Management
- Screen Printing and Hand Painting on Glass
- Soap and Detergents
- Sports Goods
- Steel Fabrication

- T.V Repairing
- Testing of Chemicals
- Tool and Die Making
- Tour Operators
- Two Wheeler Maintenance & Repair
- Wax Candle and Chalk Crayons
- Wireman Training
- 2D
- 3D
- Adobe
- Advance JAVA
- Autodesk Combustion
- CC++ and OOPs
- Computer Hardware and Networking
- Core JAVA
- Digital Photography & Videography
- Electronic Mechanic
- Engineering Drawing with CAD
- Finishing & Packing Supervisor
- Fitter Fabrication
- Fitter Maintenance General
- Housekeeping & Hospitality
- Interior Design
- Landscape Design
- Linux Administration
- MCP and CCNA
- Medical Transcription
- MS Office and Internet
- Multimedia and Animation
- Net Programming
- O Level (DOEACC)
- OOPs through JAVA
- Programming & Operation for Computerized Numerically Controlled
- Receptionist
- Routing Technology CCNA
- Security Guard
- SQL Server Database Administration
- TIG/MIG Welding
- Visual Effects
- Web Designing
- Basic Hydraulics
- Basic Pneumatics
- CAD with Pro Engineers
- Dot Net Technology
- Graphics Design
- IT Tools and Applications
- Maintenance Fitter
- Material Testing
- PC Maintenance
- Sheet Metal Worker
- Welder
- Auto Body Painting
- Diesel Fuel Injection Technician
- Maintenance Battery
- Repair and Maintenance of PA and Audio
- Repair and Maintenance of Power supply, Inverter and UPS
- Repair and Maintenance of Washing Machine and Microwave Oven
- Repairing of Auto Air Conditioning
- Repair and Maintenance of Intercom System

Training of Trainors

- Technology Infusion cum Skill Development Programme
- TOT in Entrepreneurship & Skill Development in 2D Animation
- TOT in ESDP for Fashion Designing
- Training of Trainers (EDP)
- Accreditation Programme for EM Trainers

Management Development Programs

- Advanced Skill for Effective Office & Change Management
- Advanced Skills for Effective Executive Secretaries and Change
- Management
- Business Advisors' Training Programme
- Business Development Plan for Micro & Small Enterprise
- Capacity Building of Principals of ITIs
- Carbon Trading
- Competency Building for Improved Performance
- Contemporary Human Resource Management Practices
- Cost Effectiveness in Economic Downturn
- Delayed Payments to MSEs
- Executive Development Programme on Achievement Motivation Training
- Export Procedures, Documentation and Management
- Extension Motivation Programme for Executives
- Finance for Non-Finance Executives
- Financial Statement Analysis
- IPR Challenges and Prospects for MSMEs
- IPR for Competitive Advantage
- ISO 9001:2008 Certification Process – Issues & Challenges
- Logistics & Supply Chain Management and Retail Management
- Marketing for Managers
- MDP on Project Management for Small Business Enterprises in Tribal
- Areas
- Modern Office Practice
- Product Identification & Marketing Strategies
- Productivity, Quality & Lean Manufacturing
- Project Appraisal
- Project Identification and Preparation of Project Profiles

- Project Preparation Skills for Micro-Enterprises through SHGs
- Strengthening Self-Help Groups for Urban Development Officials (under SJSRY)

Others Skill India Courses

- Assessment of SHGs for Promotion of Micro Enterprises
- Cluster Development
- Entrepreneurship & Skill Development for Partner Organistions/Agencies
- Financing & Management of CFCs
- Lending Strategies for MSMEs
- Orientation Programme for Officials of Industries & Commerce
- Department
- Orientation to Skill & Entrepreneurship Development under SJRY,
- PMEGP etc.
- Promotion of Induced Clusters
- Promotion of Micro-Enterprises
- Promotion of Service Enterprises
- Promotion of Viable Enterprises for SHGs
- Risk Management for SHGs
- Union Budget and MSMEs

References

Adams, *AA* (2012). *The Role of Skill Development in Overcoming Skill Disadvantage.* UNESCO

A B D (2015). *Challenges and Opportunities for Skill Development in Asia.*

Autor, DH., Levy, F and Murane (2003).The Skill Content of Recent Technological change: An Emprical Exploration. *Quarterly Journal of Economics*, 118 (4).

Dahiman, C and Anju, U (2005). *India and the Knowledge Economy: Leveraging Strengths and Opportunities.* Washington: World Bank.

European Commission (2010). *New Skills for New Jobs: Action Now: A Report by the Expert Group.*

FICCI (2013). *Knowledge Paper on Skill Development in India: Global Skill Summit*

Govt of India (2009). *Skill Formation and Employment Assurance in the Unorganised Sector.* New Delhi: National Commision for Enterprises in the Unorganised Sector.

Govt of India (2004). *India Vision.* New Delhi: Planning Commission

ILO (2010). *Skilled Workforce for Strong, Sustainable and Balanced Growth: A G20 Training Strategy.*

ILO (2013). Skill *Development Initiative: Modular Employable Skills Scheme: Feedback from the Field.*

ILO (2011). *Formulating a National Policy on Skill Development.*

ILO (2008). *Skills for Improved Productivity, Employment Growth and Development.*

Ministry of Labour and Employment (2009). *National Skill Development Policy* New Delhi: Govt of India

Ministry of Skill Development and Entrepreneurship (2015). *National Policy for Skill Development and Entrepreneurship – 2015. New Delhi:* Govt of India

Middleton, J Ziderman and Adams, A (1993). *Skills for Productivity: Vocational Education and Training in Developing Countries.* New York: OUP.

Mehoratra, S., Ankit, G and Bimal, KS (2013) *Estimating the Skill Gap on a Realistic Basis for 2022.* New Delhi: IAMR & PC.

NITI AAYOG (2015). *Report of the Sub-Group of Chief Ministers on Skill Development.* New Delhi: Govt of India

Nanda, R (2017). Paradigm Shift Towards Skill Development and Entrepreneurship. *University News,* 55 (07)

NSDC (2014). *The Aspiring Youth: Opportunities and Challenges of Skill Development in India.* New Delhi: Govt of India

NSDC (2013). *Approach Paper for Setting up sector skill Councils.* New Delhi: Govt of India

National Skill Development Agency (2014). *Skill Development Landscape in India.* New Delhi: New Century Publications.

Pandya, R (2016). *Skill Development and Entrepreneurship in India.* New Delhi: Vedam Books.

Sharma, R K (2010). *UGC Schemes for Vocational Education and Skill Development In* ndia. New Delhi: Arise Publications

Sing, U K (2016). Government Vision on Skill Development. *Yojana* September 2016

Sudarshan, R M (2012). *National Skill Development Strategies and the Urban Informal Sector,* UNESCO.

Saini, V (2015). Skill Development in India: Need, challenges and ways Forward. *Abhinv National Monthly,* 4(4).

Srinivasan, S (2013). *Skill Development Initiative in India.* Singapore: Institute of South Asian Studies.

UKIERI (2015). *Skill Development Landscape in India: a Perspective for Foreign Service Providers.*

Index